George Orwell
A political life

LIVES of the LEFT is a series of original biographies of leading figures in the European and North American socialist and labour movements. Short, lively and accessible, they are welcomed by students of history and politics and by everyone interested in the development of the Left.

general editor David Howell

J. Ramsay MacDonald Austen Morgan
R. H. Tawney Anthony Wright
Thomas Johnston Graham Walker
Arthur Henderson Fred Leventhal
William Lovett Joel Wiener
John Maclean Brian Ripley and John McHugh
John Strachey Mike Newman
Daniel De Leon Stephen Coleman
John Wheatley Ian Wood
George Lansbury Jonathan Schneer
John Reed Eric Homberger
J. A. Hobson Jules Townshend
Tom Mann Joseph White
Ernest Bevin Peter Weiler
Walter Reuther Anthony Carew

George Orwell
A political life

Stephen Ingle

MANCHESTER UNIVERSITY PRESS
Manchester and New York

distributed exclusively in the USA and Canada by St. Martin's Press

Copyright © Stephen Ingle 1993

Published by Manchester University Press
Oxford Road, Manchester M13 9PL, UK
and Room 400, 175 Fifth Avenue, New York, NY 10010, USA

Distributed exclusively in the USA and Canada
by St. Martin's Press, Inc., 175 Fifth Avenue, New York,
NY 10010, USA

British Library Cataloguing-in-Publication Data

Ingle, Stephen.
  George Orwell: a political life/Stephen Ingle.
    p.   cm. — (Lives of the left)
  Includes index.
    ISBN 0–7190–3233–4 (hardback)
    1. Orwell, George. 1903–1950—Political and social views.
  2. Politics and literature—England—History—20th century.
  3. Great Britain—Politics and government—20th century.   I. Title.
  II. Series.
  PR6029.R8Z7116   1993
  828'.91209—dc20   92–26932

Library of Congress Cataloging-in-Publication Data applied for

ISBN 0 7190 3233 4 *hardback*

Printed in Great Britain
by Bookcraft (Bath) Ltd.

Contents

	Foreword	*page* vii
	Preface	viii
1	**The recusant**	I
2	**The nether world**	15
3	**The politics of decency**	36
4	**The world set free**	57
5	**The politics of ideology**	83
6	**Orwellian socialism today**	107
	References	134
	Index	143

FOR JOE, BEN AND CASSIE

Foreword

For a number of years I have been teaching a course entitled 'Politics and Literature' in which Orwell has featured prominently. Although by no means unique, such a course is nevertheless a rarity in a politics department. This course was the direct consequence (and hence this book the indirect consequence) of the promptings of friends and colleagues at the University of Hull, Noel O'Sullivan and the late and much missed Bob Berki. I have them to thank for the discovery of an area of the study of politics which became a consuming interest for me. I did much of the writing at the University of Stirling in a lively and supportive intellectual atmosphere amidst inspirational country.

While I was working on this book my father died after a long and distressing illness. He was a working man, brought up in a large family, and born not many years after Orwell. He was one of those about whom Orwell wrote. My own upbringing in an extended working-class family led me to recognise that the values that Orwell claimed to have seen in working-class communities were not just the fruits of a solitary and romantic imagination; they were actually the stuff of life for those fortunate enough to have been born into such an environment. Although Orwell's ideas deserve to be discussed with critical detachment, it is proper that I declare my position. Whether they have survived into our own times or not, whether they formed a viable basis for politics or not, Orwellian values *did* exist: I saw them.

Preface

This age makes me so sick that I sometimes am almost impelled to stop at a corner and start calling down curses from Heaven like Jeremiah or Ezra or something. George Orwell, 1935.

George Orwell was certainly not the most productive of writers. He died at the age of forty-six and had suffered from intermittent ill-health for much of his adult life. Moreover, fame came late; it was Orwell's penultimate book, *Animal Farm*, which made his name, and in doing so not only ensured the eager anticipation of his next and last book, *Nineteen Eighty-four*, but also a reassessment of his earlier work. In fact posterity became so interested in Orwell that a four-volume edition of his collected essays, letters and journalism was published a quarter of a century after his death. By 1984, Orwell's *Nineteen Eighty-four* was selling 50,000 copies a day in the United States, and that same year 27 per cent of Americans claimed to have read it. In Britain, sales of the book approached half a million, and *Animal Farm* proved almost as popular. Phrases such as 'double-think', 'Big Brother is watching you', 'all animals are equal but . . .' have become part of the language, and not only the English language.[1]

The interest in Orwell is not so much due to his prose style, highly regarded though this is, but in his political commentary: it is primarily for his politics that Orwell is remembered. The quality of Orwell's writing is an important consideration, in that it provided him with a ready means of communicating successfully to a very wide readership. But that quality of prose seemed to be directly related to the political purpose of the writer – and this was no mere accident. Orwell elucidated four motives for writing, which he believed were to be found in every writer, though in different proportions. These were: sheer egoism (the desire to be remembered after one's death and talked about during one's lifetime); aesthetic enthusiasm (a perception of beauty, a pleasure taken in the juxtaposition of sounds, in a sense of rhythm, in a desire to share important aesthetic experiences); a 'desire to see things as they are, to find out true facts and to store them up for the use of posterity'; and finally political purpose (the desire to 'alter other people's ideas of the kind of society they should strive after').

Orwell suggests that these impulses don't always pull in the same direction, indeed they may sometimes be at war with each other. He believed that his own personal involvement in the Spanish civil war had weighted the balance decisively as far as he was concerned towards the third and especially the fourth impulse. He went so far as to suggest that in an overtly political age such as the 1930s any writer who ignored politics was 'either a footler or a plain idiot', and believed that if he had lived at another time he would have concerned himself much more with aesthetics. Most commentators believe that it was Orwell's intense political commitment that breathed life into his writing; it did not, as he suggests, *prevent* him from becoming a great writer, but actually *made* him a great writer. In fact, as his career progressed Orwell sought increasingly to fuse aesthetic and political purpose. There are very few critics indeed who would doubt his triumphant success; that is why Orwell continues to be so widely read.

Perhaps strangely, in view of what we have already said, there is no generally accepted view of what Orwell's politics actually were. Indeed there are those who would argue that Orwell's was by no means a 'life of the left'. Orwell himself, however, declared that 'every line I write, I write for democratic socialism as I understand it'; this claim will be considered in some detail, as will the development of his socialism through the 1930s and 1940s, in an effort to try to discover how and why it changed. The extent to which the common threads running through his writing may be considered to form a coherent political philosophy will also be examined. Finally, the relevance of Orwell's philosophy to the development of British socialism and specifically to the British Labour party in the 1990s will be assessed.

This study comprises six chapters: the first deals with Orwell's background and his reaction to it. As a young man Orwell saw the world as being divided between exploiters and exploited. His family background and education show clearly that, in his own terms, Orwell was an exploiter. His attempts to distance himself from his background and to establish his credentials as one of the exploited will be examined.

Chapter 2 considers in more detail Orwell's attempt to associate himself with the exploited, to understand their philosophy. It follows his journey to the 'bedrock of western civilization'. Orwell analyses the nature of extreme poverty but finds no philosophy more enduring than the simple establishment of priorities, such as solving the problem of where the next meal is to come from.

The third chapter focuses on Orwell's trip to the north of England to undertake a survey of poverty for the publisher Victor Gollancz. Among the working classes in the North, Orwell believed that he had found what he took to be a philosophy, an enduring attitude to life and to social relations, which he equated with socialism. Orwell saw this philosophy put to the test in the Spanish civil war, and his conclusions will be discussed.

Chapter 4 considers Orwell's view of the place of revolution in the development of socialism. His apparent espousal, and then ultimate rejection, of violent revolution as a way forward is an important element of his thinking and encompasses that period of his life when Orwell began to gain international acclaim as a writer.

Chapter 5 looks at Orwell's attitude towards political ideologies and considers the charge against intellectuals that if they involve themselves in politics they have a propensity towards totalitarianism. Orwell's fierce denunciation of the Soviet Union is well known but is often seen out of context, for he was concerned to expose the totalitarian propensity of every ideology. British socialism, as exemplified by influential thinkers like Shaw and Wells, was by no means exempt from this, and Orwell established this case to such an extent that many believed him to have become an enemy of socialism.

The final chapter attempts to draw some conclusions, by identifying Orwellian socialism and showing it to be rooted in working-class culture, strongly egalitarian, anti-revolutionary, anti-élitist, and anti-ideology. Finally, the relevance of Orwellism in the context of modern British socialism, especially in the current search of the British Labour Party to find new forms of socialism will be assessed.

One word more. There have been two official 'lives' of Orwell, one written in 1980 and one in 1991, both substantial works and both major research enterprises. There have also been a considerable number of 'unofficial' biographies. I make no claim to be providing new information about Orwell's life. My intention is to provide a detailed analysis of the development of Orwell's thought, and the chronology of his life is important only as a framework for that development. Orwell was a man who devoured and was devoured by political ideas. It is highly appropriate, therefore, that his place among the 'Lives of the Left' should be a political life.

A kilometre away the Ministry of Truth, Winston's place of work, towered vast & white over the landscape. This, he thought, was the chief of the most popular of the provinces of Oceania, wondered vaguely whether it had always been quite like this — these vistas of rotting nineteenth-century houses, their sides shored up with baulks of timber, their windows patched with cardboard, soggy in all directions; & the bombed sites where the plaster dust swirled in the air & the willowherb straggled over the heaps of rubble; & the places where the bombs had cleared a larger patch & there had sprung up sordid colonies of wooden dwellings like chicken houses. The Ministry of Truth, however — Minitrue, to give it its Newspeak name — differed from all others an enormous pyramidal structure of glittering white concrete, soaring up, terrace after terrace after terrace, three hundred metres into the air. From where Winston was standing it was just possible to read, picked out on its white face in elegant lettering, the three slogans of the Party:

WAR IS PEACE
FREEDOM IS SLAVERY
IGNORANCE IS STRENGTH.

The Ministry of Truth contained, it was said, three thousand rooms above ground level, & even vaster ramifications below. whole of three other buildings of similar size & appearance. If you climbed out the roof of Victory Mansions, it was possible to see all four of them simultaneously. The Ministry of Truth concerned itself with news, propaganda, education & the fine arts. The Ministry of Peace concerned itself with

Newspeak was the official language of Oceania. For an account of its grammar & etymology, see Appendix. O.P.

Photograph of George Orwell © Mrs Fierz

←

Manuscript page, draft of *Nineteen Eighty-Four* and photograph of George Orwell (1936). Reproduced by kind permission of the George Orwell Archive, University College London

1 The recusant

George Orwell, who liked to impress his friends by drinking his tea from a saucer, was brought up in a family unlikely to have encouraged such behaviour. His father was a civil servant in India, trained for membership in the administrative middle-class of imperialist Britain. Richard Walmsley Blair was the tenth and youngest child of a Dorset vicar who devoted his life to an undistinguished and somewhat obscure branch of the Indian civil service, the opium department. It was, as its title suggests, the job of that department to oversee the production, collection and transportation of Indian opium to China. This trade produced a profit equivalent to approximately one-sixth of the entire government revenue in India, but its function was to help perpetuate 'one of the worst evils of the British colonial system'.[1] Richard Blair began his career as an assistant sub-deputy agent grade three, and travelled around the country stations of rural India for twenty years. In 1896, at the age of thirty-nine, he married Ida Mabel Limouzin, daughter of a French father and English mother who had grown up in Moulmein, Burma, where her father was a teak merchant.

Orwell was his parents' second child, born Eric Arthur Blair in Motihari, Bengal, on June 25 1903. His elder sister, five years his senior, was called Marjorie. Before Eric reached his second birthday, Ida Blair chose to return to England to plan for life after her husband's retirement seven years later. The family settled in Henley, where their second daughter, Avril, was born in 1908. Eric was a lonely child who did not enjoy the best of health.[2] He saw very little of his father, who spent only one spell of leave at home before retiring. According to Michael Shelden, one of Orwell's biographers, the young Eric became friendly with the children of a local plumber; but his mother disapproved, and forbade him to continue seeing them. Perhaps, Shelden suggests, she discovered the children had been experimenting sexually, or perhaps she was simply being snobbish. At any rate, as an adult Orwell was to remember and reflect upon this separation.

Eric's early schooling was at a small local Anglican convent school, and at the age of eight, a year or so before his father's return, he was sent to St Cyprian's, a boarding school near Eastbourne in Sussex, which Orwell later immortalised in his essay 'Such, Such Were the Joys'.[3] Eric spent five unhappy years in an environment which possessed most of the vices and precious few of the virtues of a British 'prep' school. We shall be looking at Orwell's account of these times later, but for the present we must try to build as objective a picture as possible of his school days.

Orwell was not the only former pupil of St Cyprian's to earn his living as a writer and to write about his school days. Cyril Connolly's account in *Enemies of Promise* is as vitriolic as Orwell's:

> Muscle-bound with character the alumni of St Wulfric's [St Cyprian's] would pass on to the best public schools, reporting their best friends for homosexuality and seeing them expelled, winning athletic distinctions . . . and prizes, and scholarships and shooting competitions as well . . . and then find their vocation in India, Burma, Nigeria and the Sudan, administering with Roman justice those natives for whom the final profligate overflow of Wulfrician character was all that time predestined.[4]

There are accounts by apologists too, such as the famous golfer Henry Longhurst, and a number of surviving letters which Eric wrote home, which, together with the memories of close friends, allow us to build up a fairly reliable picture of the young Eric Blair. He seems to have enjoyed and suffered in about equal proportions, being proud of his academic achievements, and enthusiastically telling his mother about 'footer' matches. Stansky and Abrahams tell us Eric's letters home exhibited 'the ordinariness of the schoolboy life described in an ordinary toughness – with a full quota of jolly chaps and ripping games of footer'.[5]

On the other hand, Eric despised the rote learning and cramming by means of which the school hoped to gain scholarship places at Britain's more prestigious public schools. The son of the proprietors of the school, who attended for one year and was a class ahead of Blair, remembered him as 'a pretty bright boy and likely to get a scholarship, but he didn't have any notable characteristics. He was, to my mind, just one of the chaps.'[6] However, as he developed into a non-sporty scholarship boy, this made Orwell an obvious target for bullying. He was, said one contemporary, 'mobbed' by the school's gang of philistines, his moon-shaped face 'too often streaked with tears'.[7] Orwell was later to claim that he had been bullied by the proprietors, but there is no unambiguous evidence to support this. There can be little doubt, however, that Blair, even at this age, was not a 'clubbable' individual and he would have made no effort to ingratiate himself with the proprietors. It is not difficult to believe that sturdy independence may have been taken for ingratitude and intellectual arrogance, and been treated accordingly. St Cyprian's regime was a tough one. Even its champion Longhurst recalls 'the cold pewter bowls of porridge with the thick shiny lumps, into which I was actually sick one day and made to stand at a side table and eat it up'.[8] Indeed, Longhurst was to quote only half-jokingly an old boy of the school who attributed his success at having 'emerged absolutely sane and fit from five years as a prisoner of war' entirely to having been at St Cyprian's.[9] Eric Blair was hardly likely to have taken much consolation from such a testimony – George Orwell even less.

Summer holidays before the war were spent in Cornwall, but in the late summer of 1916 Eric met the Buddicom children whose acquaintance was greatly to enrich his holidays. Jacintha Buddicom came to know Eric well during his school years; they were, she said, 'twin souls'. Her recollections of Eric at this time are illuminating. She is clear that Blair had no special animosity towards his school. 'There were things he didn't like about it, but then, boys don't very often care for their prep schools . . . No, I think he had a very normal childhood.'[10] Blair's holiday activities, says Buddicom, were much more to his liking. There were frequent fishing and shooting trips with her brothers, and when the weather was wet the boys would become involved with chemistry, on one occasion managing to blow off their eyebrows. George Bowling, in *Coming Up for Air*, tried to recapture Eric's pre-war youthful world in Lower Binfield: 'There was no harping on inferiority and poverty by Eric *then* . . . The picture painted of a wretched little neurotic, snivelling miserably before a swarm of swanking bullies, suspecting that he "smelt", just was not Eric at all.'[11] Humphrey Dakin, who was to marry Eric's sister Marjory, gives a somewhat different picture again: 'A rather nasty little fat boy with a constant grievance. It took him a long time to grow out of it.'[12]

In 1917, having narrowly missed a scholarship to Eton, Blair was invited to take up a place there anyway, though he spent an unhappy term at Wellington before going. St Cyprian's declared a full day's holiday in celebration. Bernard Crick concludes of these early years: 'The main point, however, is that taking holidays as well as school, freedom as well as constraint, no terrible harm seems to have been done.'[3]

Blair went to Eton a self-confident, intelligent, widely-read boy who had clearly enjoyed the benefits of a privileged childhood. He was, moreover, moved by much the same feelings as his peers, even though he was clearly better able to express them: the *Henley and Slough Oxfordshire Standard* of 2 October 1914 published a poem by the eleven-year-old Eric entitled 'Awake! Young Men of England'. What set Blair apart was no physical weakness or a battered psyche but the firm conviction that he would become a famous writer. 'He was always going to write', says Jacintha Buddicom, 'and he was always going to be a Famous Writer . . . That was his trade mark, "Eric the Famous Writer".'[4]

Blair was a King's scholar, and thus was part of an intellectual élite and, much more important to his parents, charged only a quarter of full fees. Contemporaries who have written about Blair all seem to agree that he was a 'thinker' rather than a 'doer': 'he'd soon developed a kind of aloofness which left him on good terms with everyone without being the close friend of any'.[5] He played little sport, though he did feature in the celebrated Eton wall game, a kind of mass rugby whose chief characteristic, beyond making participants unrecognisably muddy, is that it has not produced a result for over eighty years. He was described by one contemporary as large and well-built though casual in manner and somewhat soft looking. Despite his earlier patriotic poetry, he was not a keen member of the Officers' Training Corps. But he was not a rebel, indeed was described as sardonic rather then rebellious, and as 'standing aside from things a bit, observing – always observing'; though as Bernard Crick has remarked Eton was not short of 'loners'.[6] If he did dislike the discipline of the Corps though, Blair characteristically proved himself, in the words of one fellow trainee officer, an 'admirable stablemate under dripping canvas'.

One activity in which Blair did engage was the production of a magazine, though – remarkably – he was the business manager of this venture. One of his co-producers remembers Blair as a boy who loved arguing. 'I remember when . . . we were introduced to Plato . . . the Platonic dialogue, in which Socrates argues like anything with a lot of other people, proving them endlessly wrong, really in order to get them *thinking*. I remember thinking, this man's just like Eric Blair.'[17] Shelden has provided new information on Blair's adolescent sexuality,[18] though whether this information amounts to any great insight is open to question.

Academically Blair's career at Eton was a failure, and he chopped and changed his studies with little success. There seems to be a general agreement that he made little effort to succeed. One contemporary wrote of Orwell that although he put little effort into academic work, he certainly read widely. He read the entire works of Shaw and Wells and was thought to 'see himself as a bit of a Bernard Shaw'.[19] In fact most of Blair's contemporaries remark upon his breadth of reading, especially of the modern 'socialist' writers. His devotion to Shaw, as to Wells and Jack London, had much to do with the urgency of their style; they were not writing for fellow-intellectuals.

A close friend of Eric's during his later years at Eton was Sir Steven Runciman, who was convinced that Blair had set his mind fairly early on going back to the East and, as a consequence, made no effort to direct his energies towards university entrance. 'He used to talk about the East a great deal, and I always had the impression he was longing to go back there. I mean it was a sort of romantic idea . . . So I wasn't in the least bit surprised that he decided to go back there instead of a university, particularly as he used to say he didn't much want to go to university.'[20]

According to Crick, at the end of his final year at Eton Blair was placed 138th out of 167 boys, which hardly supports Buddicom's view – completely at odds with Runciman's – that Blair wanted very much to go up to Oxford and was merely pretending to fit in with his father's scheme of a future with the Indian Civil Service. It is just possible that all along Orwell had been making a virtue of necessity, pretending a love for the East because he knew of his father's intentions. On the other hand, had he truly wished to go on to university he would scarcely have finished near the bottom of his election. His classics tutor Andrew Gow (who was to visit him not long before Orwell died) declared that there had never been any question of Richard Blair's being in a position to fund his son at university, and that Eric had 'not the faintest hope' of gaining a scholarship.[21] Since he had exhibited little enthusiasm for rigorous academic study, and since he intended to write, it is logical to conclude that Buddicom was mistaken and that Orwell had settled for going out East. In fact he was successful in the examinations for the Imperial Police. Shelden argues that Mrs Blair was even keener for her son to go to Burma than his father was. Both would have regarded the Imperial Police as a highly prestigious career.

Whatever his motivation, Blair left Britain in October 1922, still only nineteen years old. He reached Rangoon in November and was soon sent to the Burma provincial police training school in Mandalay. His first posting took him to a small town on the Irrawaddy delta, where he ran the headquarters office and arranged for the policing of the locality. He was moved on after only three months, to a more rural location – hardly promotion. His third posting was to the Burmah Oil Company's refinery at Syriam, where he was responsible for the security of the refinery. It was a posting Blair keenly disliked, though he was obliged to stay for nine months before moving to Burma's third-largest town, Moulmein. Although in all respects a more congenial posting, Blair seems by this time to have become thoroughly disenchanted with the service. His maternal grandmother was living in Moulmein at the time and it seems likely he would have visited the Limouzins though there is no record of this. (Indeed, if Crick is right in identifying aspects of Mrs Limouzin in the character of Mrs Lackersteen in *Burmese Days* then Blair certainly did not care much for his Moulmein relations, and is unlikely to have been a frequent visitor.[22]

All in all Orwell felt himself isolated, from his fellow ex-patriots, from the local Burmese and perhaps above all from the values of imperialism. The extent to which this isolation was self-inflicted is debatable. Certainly the pictures that others had of Blair were by no means unambiguous. One Burman who made enquiries about Blair in Moulmein following the publication of *Burmese Days* discovered 'only a handful of people [who] could remember anything about him, and they remembered him merely as a sporting and skilful centre-forward who scored many goals for the Moulmein police team'.[23] Most who knew him well found him a lugubrious young man, with no taste for the club-life that was the cornerstone of ex-patriot existence, but not noticeably a rebel. Etonian friend Christopher Hollis met Blair in Burma on his way to Australia, and noted his obvious unhappiness. Blair seemed, he said, to be a man divided between the conventional imperial policeman and the radical critic of imperialism. There was little doubt, though, that by the end of his first term of duty Blair had lost the necessary self-confidence of the former, and his regard for the culture of the native Burmese drew him increasingly towards the latter. He would attend services in Burmese temples and talk with the priests in their own language, distressing colleagues, who suspected him of 'going native'. Although there is no evidence of his having a long-term Burmese lover, like his hero Flory, it was common knowledge that he had had sexual relations with Burmese women, [24] and indeed Shelden thinks there may have been a relationship with a European woman similar to that between Flory and Elizabeth. [25]

Blair's growing dislike of his life in Burma is even more easily understood if we grant his earlier enthusiasm for Asian culture as genuine and not simply making a virtue of family necessity. His letters to Jacintha Buddicom give testimony to his feelings: 'I don't think that when he first went out Eric realised how much he'd hate it when he got there. I don't really know why he did hate it so much, but he did. He thought it was absolutely frightful . . . .' [26] It is surprising, all things considered, that Blair stayed so long. Probably the humiliation of an immediate return was too much to contemplate, and perhaps after getting through his training year successfully life became a little more bearable. In addition the job involved considerable responsibility. At the age of twenty-one he was in charge of a local force of nearly 200 men and was responsible for guarding an industrial area and enforcing the law: he was, in short, 'overseeing life-and-death matters for a population which was equal to that of a medium-sized European city'. [27] In 1927, following a painful and depressing attack of dengue, Blair successfully applied for a few months' leave before his five-year term was due to end. He left Burma and returned to Britain.

By the time of his return 'one sniff of English air' finally persuaded him to resign. Blair's family had settled in Suffolk, in the seaside town of Southwold, but Eric found the town little to his liking. Moreover, his decision to forsake the Imperial Police displeased his father and created something of a barrier between them. Eric's younger sister Avril spoke of an additional problem caused by Blair's having become accustomed to being waited upon and not having made the adjustments appropriate to his new life at home. Even without these problems, however, it is not easy to imagine Eric settling to English small-town life with its rigid social stratification. (The family tailor, who served them for years, would not be 'recognised' by Eric's father if they happened to meet around town.)

7

No surprise, then, that Blair did not stay long in Southwold but instead began his sorties into the East End of London – dressed as a tramp. Soon, in the spring of 1928, he left for Paris, where he was to spend more than a year living and working among the poor. He had finally decided to make a career as a writer, and to adopt a way of life from which he was not to depart to any great extent for the rest of his life.

Why did he do it? Why did he choose to 'go native' in his own country? To put the question another way: why did Eric Blair choose to take the first step to becoming George Orwell? We will look at these questions again in chapter 2, but first, it will be helpful to look at the major works which cover this early period of Orwell's life.

Orwell's experiences in Burma were later to be recorded in his novel, *Burmese Days*, published by Gollancz in 1935. The story concerns a small outpost in Upper Burma – Kyauktada – and a young timber merchant, John Flory, and his relations with the ex-patriot community. Flory is the archetypal Orwellian hero, an outsider whose status as such is indicated by a disfiguring birthmark on one side of his face – a physical manifestation of his alienation from society according to Lee.[28] His friendship with an Indian doctor in the community earns him not only the contempt of the ex-pats at the local club but also enmeshes him, unknowingly, in the machinations of a ruthlessly ambitious Burmese magistrate, U Po Kyin. The club at Kyauktada is advised to give membership to an Asian, as part of government policy, and U Po Kyin has set his sights on being that member. Veraswami – the doctor befriended by Flory – is his only competitor, and the magistrate sets about discrediting Veraswami, and in the end Flory, in order to achieve his purpose. Flory, too, has an objective: to marry Elizabeth, the niece of the Lackersteens, an attractive but small-minded young woman who takes Flory seriously only after the departure from Kyauktada of an arrogantly patrician military policeman who possesses all the social graces and martial virtues that Flory lacks.

Flory's marital prospects are suddenly improved when he is instrumental in putting down a minor revolt which threatened the club. His equally sudden humiliation and disgrace are engineered by U Po Kyin. Elizabeth spurns him and Flory takes his own life. Without the support of his European friend, Veraswami is undermined by the magistrate, and U Po Kyin achieves his objective of membership of the club and indeed all his ambitions. This is a story without heroes, a story of mendacity, treachery and hypocrisy, of racial and social repression and hatred.

The story provides the author with the opportunity to expose the imperial élite to ruthless analysis. Among the ex-pats is Ellis, an intelligent and able timber executive, who had for all Asians 'a bitter, restless loathing as of something evil and unclean . . . any hint of friendly feeling towards an Oriental seemed to him a horrible perversity'.[29] Ellis's feelings are roused to fury by a government policy of encouraging the admittance of non-Europeans to clubs. Rounding on Flory, whose friendship with doctor Veraswami is well known, Ellis remarks: ' Do what you like outside the club. But, by God, it's a different matter when you talk of bringing niggers in here . . . By God, he'd go out with my boot behind him if ever I saw his black snout inside that door.' Orwell makes it clear that Ellis's attitude may be paranoid but it is not without some imperialist rationale: 'Here we are, supposed to be governing a set of damned black swine who've been slaves since the beginning of history, and instead of ruling them in the only way they understand, we go and treat them as equals.'[30]

Among the ex-pats only the Lackersteens are as fully drawn as Ellis, and Orwell's attitude to the wife has already been alluded to. Her views on race relations in Burma signal that Orwell was already making connections between overseas and domestic 'imperialism': 'Really I think the laziness of these servants is getting too shocking,' she complained. 'We seem to have no *authority* over the natives nowadays, with all those dreadful Reforms, and the insolence they learn from the newspapers. In some ways they are getting almost as bad as the lower classes at home.'[31] As for Lackersteen himself, he is shown to be a drunkard and a lecher, part of an empire described by Flory as cemented together by booze.

Flory declares his position to be not anti-empire but anti-humbug. He, too, wants to make money but not to the extent of participating in the 'slimy white-man's burden' hypocrisy. Let's not pretend, he argues, that the white man is in Burma to uplift the Burmese; he is there to rob them. Living the imperial pretence 'corrupts us . . . There's an everlasting sense of being a sneak and a liar that torments us and drives us to justify ourselves night and day.'[32] The whole business of empire, Flory concludes, may be summed up as follows: 'The official holds the Burman down while the businessman goes through his pockets.'[33] This, says Flory, is the Pox Britannica.

Such an unremitting onslaught seems almost Shavian in tone, especially in claiming to attack hypocrisy rather than empire. Orwell knew, as Veraswami points out, that in building up the infrastructures of transport and communications, irrigation, health, education and the legal system of the subject nations, the imperialists *had* contributed to the well-being of those they governed. Moreover, if we are to take Flory and Orwell seriously about the targeting of hypocrisy, we would expect a more tolerant appraisal of Ellis, whose position is anything but hypocritical. In reality Flory deludes himself, for at base the hypocrisy he attacks is nothing more than the lubricant of the imperial machine, allowing enthusiastic and reluctant imperialists to convince themselves that they are involved in a mighty enterprise for the good of all. That 'hypocrisy' was the difference between the Raj and the East India Company, the difference between the British empire in the East and the Japanese. By claiming to attack hypocrisy rather than empire, Orwell seems to have made use of Blair's trick of standing on his head to attract attention.

At root Orwell is critical of a system in which louts fresh from school (where the school song would be something like Flory's, *The Scrum of Life*), would kick grey-haired servants, a system in which not only the natives have no liberty but also the masters. Free speech is impossible when every white man is a cog in the wheels of despotism. The only freedoms that existed for the masters were the freedom to drink and to fornicate. All other actions and thoughts were dictated by the code of the *sahiblog*. Unlike Winston Smith, who finds a revolutionary soulmate, Flory finds that 'in the end the secrecy of your revolt poisons you like a secret disease'.[34] Small wonder that Eric Blair, whose experiences and perceptions shaped this remorselessly bitter novel, decided to get out of the imperial racket. Robert Lee has argued that *Burmese Days*, like much of Orwell's work, concerns the theme of corrupted language. In the novel language fails at crucial moments, says Lee, 'in ways which suggest that merely to articulate . . . would be sufficient to prevent disaster'.[35] If this were wholly true it would surely diminish the deterministic element of a novel whose outcome, in large measure, is predictable in terms of the imperialistic relationship. Lee is clearly right to signal Orwell's deep commitment to language, but his point here is not relevant, for the constraints of language are themselves the product of that relationship and not some independent variable.

This savaging of imperialism received little reproach from 'imperialists', though the principal of the police training school in Burma was reported as exclaiming that 'if ever he met that young man again he was going to horse-whip him'.[36]

If *Burmese Days* deals with some fundamental personal issues, the more overtly political issues are handled in two essays, *Shooting an Elephant* (1936) and *A Hanging*. Both essays are clearly autobiographical, and although Bernard Crick was unable to verify that Orwell had actually participated in the events depicted, such events were themselves common enough. Autobiographical or not, the 'experiences' are used by the writer for an entirely political purpose.

The first story concerns an elephant on the rampage. A young imperial policeman is supposed to go and kill the elephant to minimise the damage it is causing – it has already killed one Indian coolie. Blair follows the trail of destruction to discover the animal in a paddy field looking no more dangerous than a cow. He realises that the elephant has not gone wild but has been subject to 'must', a sexual frenzy, which would wear off. And he also realises that to shoot the elephant would be not only unnecessary but quite immoral. But he is not a free agent; he is part of the imperial system. He is hated by the local Burmese and he himself hates them, at times feeling his greatest joy would have been 'to drive a bayonet into a Bhuddist priest's guts'. But his greatest hatred he reserves for his job – 'I hated it more bitterly than I can perhaps make clear.' And here he was, confronting a docile animal, but willed forward by the crowd, willed to kill: he the man with the rifle, with the authority, they an unarmed and apparently powerless group of natives. But in reality, he went on, 'I was only an absurd puppet pushed to and fro by the will of those yellow faces behind. I perceived in this moment that when the white man turns tyrant it is his own freedom that he destroys. He becomes a sort of hollow, posing dummy. . . .'

A Hanging is a less overtly didactic essay, dealing with the execution of a prisoner in Burma. We are not told what the man is guilty of, neither is any inference overtly drawn from the events which are described. Orwell draws the reader up sharp by his reflections on the fact that the condemned man, walking to the gallows, actually steps aside to avoid a puddle. For the first time in his life the policeman is confronted by the reality of actually killing, in cold blood, a normal, healthy man. When he sees the prisoner step aside to avoid the puddle he recognises the 'unspeakable wrongness' of taking the life of a perfectly healthy person. They were a party of men walking together, experiencing the same world; yet 'in two minutes, with a sudden snap, one of us would be gone – one mind less, one world less.' For the reader the important, untold part of the story is that 'justice' is the prerogative of the imperial power, the exploiter, and the recipient is of the exploited nation. Justice is carried out, moreover, by a disillusioned young British officer and a group of Indian soldiers whom Orwell manages to portray as lackeys, unenthusiastic for their task but anxious to win the favours of the British officer. The whole exercise, in short, was a sordid example of the exploiter/exploited ralationship that characterised imperialism.

Supporters of imperialism had always acknowledged that the white man's burden was a heavy one, entailing, in Kipling's words, 'the blame of those ye better, the hate of those ye guard'. Yet the assumption had always been that, in the long run, the relationship was of mutual benefit, bringing to the subject races all the advantages of modernisation and Christianity, and to the the imperial race not merely clear economic advantages but also the opportunity of serving the great cause of civilisation. Even many of those whose interpretation of the relationship was entirely economic were convinced that there were substantial gains for both sides (except Marxist economists of course). Orwell's view may be summarised as accepting the Marxist view of the economics of imperialism and as rejecting totally any notion of moral or cultural gains for either side: imperialism debased both sides utterly, not only in the personal and social sense, as in *Burmese Days*, but also politically, as the two short stories indicate. Both sides were obliged to adopt policies which they privately found distasteful. It is the very condition of the imperialist's rule, says Orwell, that he should spend his life in trying to impress the 'natives', and so he finds himself obliged, every day, to do what the 'natives' expect of him. He has to wear a mask and his face eventually takes on its character. So the nature of the imperialist relationship is an intensely alienating one; both sides are alienated from each other and from their roles (i.e. from themselves). What is true of imperialism is by extension true of every tyranny, indeed of every relationship involving subservience and dependency.

I have already suggested that Orwell was to apply the imperial model of power to British class relations. An excellent example of its use is provided by his account of his school days at St Cyprian's, with the ironic title, *Such, Such Were the Joys*, borrowed from Blake's *Songs of Innocence*. Although it relates to his early years, Orwell actually wrote it in the 1940s, and it represents his thinking in those later years. Here, Orwell portrays Eric not as exploiter but as exploited. Although he is at a fee-paying school he is quick to establish that his place there was at a reduced fee because he was a potential scholarship winner to Eton. The consequences of this economic fact were enormous. Although the headmaster behaved with forbearance to the sons of the wealthy — indeed Orwell declared 'I doubt whether Sambo ever caned any boy whose father's income was much above £2,000 a year' — he was almost brutal with the poorer boys. The relationship between them was economic: the boys' abilities represented a substantial long-term investment, the profits of which have to be safeguarded. Orwell claimed that the boys were continuously underfed for 'sound commercial reasons'. In depicting the relationship between staff and boys in terms of the imperialist model he shows a system ruled not by love but by fear. At a tender age boys were taken from the comfort and security of their families and dropped into a world of power relations, dishonesty and hypocrisy — 'out of a gold-fish bowl and into a tank full of pike'. What is more, Orwell observed that it was quite impossible ever to join the really wealthy. If one worked very hard one might attain a measure of comfort by middle age but 'even if you climbed to the highest niche that was open to you, you could only be an underling, a hanger-on of the people who really counted'. Again the imperial metaphor comes to mind; even U Po Kyin could not aspire to become European. Money, says Orwell, was synonymous with goodness, with moral virtue. The strong (who were the rich) always won, and since virtue was their agent, they always deserved to win. The weak (who were the poor) always lost and deserved to. Those were the rules of the exploitation game.

The accuracy of Orwell's picture of his school days is a question already touched on; nobody who knew him or the school seems to agree with him very much, or indeed with each other. Having researched the matter with great care Shelden is doubtful about much of what Orwell wrote. On the other hand, he is clearly of the view that it was not all invention. He quotes one contemporary as saying that Mrs Wilkes pulled Blair's hair so much that he deliberately kept it permanently greasy.[37] David Ogilvie, founder of an advertising agency, refers to Mrs Wilkes as a 'satanic woman'.[38] Nevertheless Blair was a promising pupil, likely to gain distinction for the school. He won several prizes and, after all, he did deliver an Eton scholarship. It seems hard to believe that a star pupil — a good investment — even if his own man, would have been treated too badly. Aldritt believes that the essay 'demonstrates more clearly [and] more succinctly the fundamental uncertainties in his mind':[39] did Orwell regard his 'problems' at school as the consequence of his own personality or of the historical situation or simply as part of the lot of children?

Perhaps these are unnecessary distinctions to draw as Orwell wished to represent each. So long as power is concentrated in a few hands the weak will suffer, and he uses his school experiences to provide an autobiographical setting for his polemic on the nature of the relationship between the powerful and the powerless. If Orwell is rewriting history, exaggerating and manipulating (but surely not inventing) accounts of beatings as punishments for bed-wetting and homosexual practices which others do not corroborate, he is rewriting it in terms of a model of exploitation which was to shape much of his later thinking. One might say that he was rewriting history to give an autobiographical authenticity to an ideology of power. Raymond Williams considered that he failed, finishing 'with the double vision, rooted in the simultaneous positions of dominator and dominated'.[40] That is one judgement, but from Orwell's point of view, the lesson to be drawn from applying his model is that the rich and the powerful (usually the same thing) are bullies, the poor and oppressed (always the same thing) noble. For the latter he has a message: 'the rules' represent nothing more than a rationalisation of the hegemony of wealth – they should break them or they will be crushed.

2 The nether world

Orwell had attempted to escape imperialism in Burma, where he was one of the oppressors, only to discover it in Britain, where he was also one of the oppressors (despite efforts to establish, through works like *Such, Such Were The Joys* that he was really one of the oppressed). Under capitalism, he concluded, the imperialist model represented the normal human condition. What to do? It was always possible to opt out of that condition altogether but it was also possible, and more useful, to attempt to opt out of one's side, one's class, and then perhaps to expose the model for what it was.

This becomes a feasible and indeed attractive proposition for him, considering his other ambition, to become a writer. He himself had parodied the attitude of *l'art pour l'art*, telling of the young man, just down from university, who announced that he intended to write and when asked about what, answered that one didn't write about anything, one simply wrote. Orwell never intended simply to write. On the other hand, setting aside his experiences in Burma, he had very little to write *from* and it was unlikely that life in Suffolk would provide him with the kind of background he sought. To leave home, to live in considerable poverty, to see the class relationship from the other side (or at least, from the outside), served both Orwell's philosophy and his ambition, though to explain this to his family was not to prove easy. However, in the autumn of 1928 Orwell moved to cheap lodgings in London, close to some friends of his parents, and began to write. 'He wrote so badly,' said one of the friends. 'He was like a cow with a musket . . . He used to put in a fair number of rude words in those days and we had to correct the spelling . . . Oh dear, I'm afraid we did laugh.'' If this sounds unlike Orwell, the picture painted of him warming his hands on a candle to be able to write through a bitterly cold winter for much of which he had no heater at all sounds more recognisable. What drove him on was the combination of ambition and philosophy. Writing later about this period in his life Orwell said: 'I was conscious of an immense weight of guilt that I had to expiate . . . I felt that I had got to escape not merely from imperialism but from every form of man's dominion over man'.[2] He wanted, he said, to live with the oppressed and share their oppression, to live with failure, and simply not to be part of the system of exploitation which he saw all around him. Success, he said, any success, was just a form of bullying.

Orwell's perception of the world and his response to it was not neurotic or even wholly psychological, but was at least in part political. He did not invent imperialism, though he *may* have embellished it somewhat in his story-telling: he did not invent the poverty in which he chose to live and millions of others were obliged to live. Even his attitude towards 'success' seems less neurotic if we bear in mind that he was not concerned with celebrity so much as money. It is not original, much less neurotic, to observe that the so-called cash-nexus is exploitative. Orwell was neither the first nor the last to accept poverty when there was an alternative. Crick argues, though, that whilst Orwell wished to distance himself from his native 'oppressor' class at this time, he had no wish actually to join the oppressed on a permanent basis, merely to observe them at close hand. Crick contends that there were purely professional considerations at work here; Orwell was looking for experience, for material for his writing. It would be nugatory to try to unravel and quantify the strength of the psychological, political and professional impulses; anyway, they pushed Orwell in the same direction and fed off each other. I believe that Orwell's political motivation, though not as strong or as well-defined as the psychological or professional, was greater than Crick would allow. It was not a philosophically coherent motivation, still less an ideological one, but in my view it represented a conscious taking of sides. At any rate – in whatever proportion – political, psychological and professional motivations prompted Orwell to make contact with those he called 'the lowest of the low'; tramps, beggars, criminals, prostitutes and the like, in an attempt to escape the respectable world. For the time being, then, Orwell is set on a voyage of discovery.

Before long Orwell set out on his first sortie into London's East End. He was not the first to have gone there on a fact-finding mission. Jack London, an author whose work had always held Orwell's imagination, had done something similar. He had come to Britain on his way to South Africa to report the Boer War, only for it to end. Instead he had spent his time on a sociological investigation of the lives of the poor of the East End, which he then wrote up in *People of the Abyss*. Bernard Shaw, too, had gone; his observations were to find literary expression in some of the characters and scenes of *Major Barbara*, with which Orwell would also have been familiar.

If this, as some have suggested, was a game for Orwell, it was a serious one; no concessions even in the coldest of winters.[3] Throughout the winter of 1927 Orwell continued his exploration, continued his writing – continued, that is, his apprenticeship. He decided, however, that come spring he would move to Paris. Nothing very unconventional about this. As Orwell himself observed, Paris was at this time 'invaded by a swarm of artists, writers, students, dilletantes, sightseers, debauchees' to the degree that they outnumbered the native population.[4] His intention was to write, and he did write copiously, but without any great success – success in the Orwellian 'bullying' sense – he didn't make any money. (However in December 1928 his first article appeared in Britain, on 'Farthing Newspapers', for *G.K.'s Weekly*.) He lived a solitary existence, not seeking to join the society of young writers and artists for which Paris seems always to have been so famous and whose company could have made life much more bearable. Orwell was later to write: 'I did just about as well as do most young people who take up a literary career – that is to say . . . my literary efforts in the first year barely brought me in twenty pounds.'[5]

What was Orwell writing about during his apprenticeship in Paris? There is little doubt that he was distilling his own experiences amongst the down-and-outs in southern England while accumulating similar material in Paris. His correspondence from these days shows him trying to place with publishers a putative book on tramps and beggars; he certainly wrote his essay 'The Spike' at this time but other essays, too, were sent out but not well received. Too little action, said a reader, too much sex.[6] It seems clear that though Orwell thought of himself at the time as a social critic, he did not see himself as a political writer in anything but the broadest terms. Crick concludes that had Orwell's work been received more fulsomely he might have remained 'in a literal and intellectual sense merely Eric Blair'.[7] This is an interesting reflection and goes to the heart of Orwell's own disquisition, discussed in the introduction, on motives for writing. Orwell, it will be remembered, felt that his political motivation had deterred his development as a more literary writer; that is to say a writer who would be remembered more for his style, for his character portrayal, for his narrative powers, than for his 'message'. It is abundantly clear, though, that it was precisely his political motivation which made Orwell a great writer. Crick is right to suggest that he was, in these early days, 'merely' Eric Blair and by the same token Crick is missing a point when he suggests that success at this stage might have hindered Orwell's development; success at this stage was not a possibility because Blair was not good enough, lucky enough or well enough connected. He needed to be politically motivated – to be Orwell – to succeed as a writer, and the progress of *Burmese Days* offers solid evidence for this argument. In its earlier forms the novel concerns drink and adultery, with the characters reacting to a life of boredom and booze. The overarching, deterministic theme of imperialism which characterises the successful novel is not there to hold the writing together and give it substance and coherence. In brief, although during these times Orwell had no success at all as a serious writer and not much as a journalist, he was beginning to establish a relationship with the material which would form the basis of so much of his later work. We shall be returning to this point.

In February 1929 Orwell contracted pneumonia and spent a short time in hospital, the experience of which he used to great effect in his later essay *How the Poor Die*. He owed this misfortune, no doubt, to working too hard in unpleasant conditions without enough to eat. His luck did not change on being discharged, for he was robbed of most of what he owned soon after, and was obliged to live on less than half his previous meagre outgoings. He had to pawn his 'decent' clothes and get a job; but of course without decent clothes he was not going to get a decent job. He finished working as a *plongeur* – a washer-up and general factotum – for thirteen hours a day towards the end of 1929. He was hardly in any position to have contemplated writing much during this time but the experiences were to provide material for his later work *Down and Out in Paris and London*.

It is often claimed that these torments in Paris were artificial in the sense that whereas for his companions the life of a scullion was 'life', for him it was 'experience', an experience from which he could have extricated himself at any time by simply contacting his Aunt Nellie, who lived in Paris and who would certainly have lent him money. Although undeniably true it is not by any means the whole truth. To have submitted himself to a life of great privation for several years, to have travelled to the 'bedrock of Western civilization' and to have clung on like a limpet despite hunger, failure and ill-health, says much for Orwell's tenacity and sense of purpose. True, millions were born to such a life and Orwell was not; they remained ensnared and he did not. Yet he sacrificed nearly every aspect of what most members of the middle class would regard as their birthright, including his health, in order to become a writer. Raymond Williams is right to insist that 'the exposure to poverty and suffering and filth and waste was as real as it was deliberate, and the record of the exposure is a remarkable enlargement of our literature'.[8] Orwell was drawn instinctively to the oppressed: he must have realised, though probably not fully conscious of the consequences, that it was oppression and its results that would provide the *leitmotif* of his work. That is to say, he must have recognised that this period in his life was an apprenticeship in much more than simply a career as a writer. When Orwell left for Southwold in time for Christmas in 1929, he could hardly have seen beyond the apparently abject failures of the years since his return from Burma. Yet he had, in fact, been making important investments upon which he was to draw for the rest of his career.

At home again, then, but only temporarily, Orwell found employment first as a tutor to a boy with learning difficulties and then to three sons of a neighbour, one of whom, Richard Peters, went on to become a Professor of Philosophy at London University's Institute of Education, and remembered Orwell with considerable affection. In the meantime he continued his writing, and by October of 1939 had completed the first draft of what was to become *Down and Out in Paris and London*. He had his essay 'The Spike' accepted for publication in *The New Adelphi* and two essays on similar themes in French journals. He was reviewing for *The New Adelphi* too, and under the guidance of the editor and his future mentor Richard Rees, was becoming a small part of the left-wing literary establishment. Left wing in the broadest sense, though, because Orwell described himself, and was described by others, as having been at the time a 'Tory anarchist'. Richard Peters remembered Orwell telling him and his brothers that, had he been alive at the time of the English Civil War, he would have sided with the Cavaliers rather than the Roundheads because the latter were such depressing people. 'Temperamentally he was a Cavalier, lacking the fervour and fanaticism of the Puritan [and the] dogmatism of the insecure.'[9]

From the spring of 1930 Orwell resumed his tramping expeditions, sometimes — and most bizarrely — setting out from Rees' Cheyne Walk flat in Chelsea, an area still popular with the Cavaliers – wealthy Conservative MPs. He also spent part of 1930 with his sister and brother-in-law in Leeds. It comes as a surprise to those who imagine that Orwell's later trip to Wigan was his first to the North to discover that he had spent some time in Yorkshire previously. Indeed, his brother-in-law frequently took him to working-class pubs in Bramley and, as Crick tells us, was not popular with the locals for doing so. Indeed, one publican actually told Orwell's brother-in-law Humphrey Dakin: 'Don't bring that bugger in here again.'[10] Dakin took Orwell's declared fellow-feeling with the working class with a pinch of salt.

The following autumn Orwell tramped to the Kentish hop-fields to work on the harvest. Until mechanisation and higher levels of disposable income, hop-picking ('oppin') provided the annual holiday for many East-End families. This experience would have provided Orwell with his first opportunity to observe at close hand the family life of the working class, and there is clear evidence that he was impressed by what he saw. In the essay 'Hop-Picking' for example, he writes:

> There was one couple, a coster and his wife, who were like a father and mother to us. They were the kind of people who are generally drunk on Saturday nights and who tack a 'fucking' on to every noun, yet I have never seen anything that exceeded their kindness and delicacy.[11]

On the other hand, Orwell was less enamoured of some of his companions and his descriptions of them clearly show that he did not always idealise the working class. Of one he wrote that he could not remember having seen anyone who disgusted him so much as this boy with his face like some 'low-down carrion-eating beast'.[12] Orwell was later to turn his hopping experiences to use in his novel *The Clergyman's Daughter*, but he came to the end of 1931 no nearer to establishing himself as a writer. Indeed success in most spheres seems to have eluded him; even his attempts to get himself arrested so as to spend Christmas in prison failed. Evidently he could not disguise his Cavalier origins from the forces of law and order, who clearly took pity on a gentleman down on his luck.

Nothing for it but to take a job again, which Orwell did, after another trip to Leeds. While there Orwell read what was later to become one of the most popular 'Roundhead' tracts, *The Ragged Trousered Philanthropists*, which he considered 'a wonderful book, although it is very clumsily written'.[13] The fact that he was recommended this book by the local librarian suggests that Orwell was actively pursuing a knowledge of working-class life and not simply trying to acquire experience from which to write. For all that, after Easter Orwell returned to the South and took up a post as teacher in charge of The Hawthorns, a very small school in Hayes. Orwell turned out to be a strict disciplinarian who possessed and frequently used a cane, but he got on well with the boys and found it easy to communicate his love for nature to them. While he was teaching at Hayes Orwell achieved his first real literary breakthrough: news came that Gollancz was to publish *Down and Out in Paris and London*, subject to certain revisions. Gollancz's reader regarded the book as an important document about the lives of the poor which should be brought to the reading public's attention. Orwell decided at this point to adopt a pseudonym under which to write, no doubt primarily to protect his family but also because he had a peculiar dislike of his own name, Eric for aesthetic reasons and Blair because it was Scottish. His adopted name was English and it was classless, and was chosen from amongst three or four possibilities suggested to Gollancz. It is interesting to speculate whether H. Lewis Allways could ever have written *Nineteen Eighty-four*! Although he did not become famous or rich as a consequence of the book's acceptance, Orwell had at long last made a breakthrough, and he clearly realised as much.

During his days at The Hawthorns there occurred what Crick refers to as an 'odd episode': Orwell started going to church. In a letter to his friend Eleanor Jaques,[14] Orwell explained his attendance as the consequence of his having befriended the curate, a 'high Anglican but not a creeping Jesus'. He also told her, however, that he could not bring himself to take Communion because he was afraid he might choke. In a subsequent letter he mentions taking the *Church Times* regularly[15] and even his decision – the danger of choking presumably having been overcome – to take Communion 'because my curate friend is bound to think it funny if I always go to Church but never communicate'.[16] This was much more than friendship could have required, and his asking Eleanor about the procedure for taking Communion because he had forgotten it seems rather fey. He was taking this interest in the Church, he said, because he had 'passed himself off as pious' and now had to take the consequences. This all seems dubious and Orwell's explanations do not add up. Crick was later to discover that Orwell's commitment went substantially further than he seemed prepared to admit to his humanist friend; he actually served at Mass (they were High Church) twice a week. Even more noteworthy perhaps, Orwell sought permission to bring church ornaments into school for the boys to redecorate; indeed he himself cleaned the crown of a statue of the Blessed Virgin with onion water.

Orwell told his humanist friend about this, explaining 'I shall try to make her look as much like one of the illustrations in La Vie Parisienne as possible.'[17] The curate and his wife were good friends of Orwell's, sharing his concern for the oppressed; indeed, they were, or were to become, socialists. It is not credible that Orwell would have cared to play such a cheap trick behind their backs. Moreover, in a letter to the co-editor of the Adelphi, Max Plowman,[18] Orwell took issue with an article in the journal which argued that religion, in concentrating on spiritual love, fixed man's desires on something unattainable, thereby causing alienation. 'The point he doesn't bring out,' argued Orwell, 'is that the "sinful lust" stuff also fixes . . . on something unattainable and can thus be even more destructive. It is important to teach boys that the heroines of Victorian literature don't exist in reality; it is just as important, and far more difficult, to teach them that women as illustrated in La Vie Parisienne don't exist either.' This completely undermines Orwell's earlier comments, exposing them as no more than the common currency of liberal humanism or an attempt at flippancy. He was clearly far more serious about these things than he was prepared to let on.

There are other examples of Orwell pursuing a keen interest in Christianity as a system of thought at this stage of his career and it is entirely reasonable to conclude that religion had become important to him. In a review written for the New English Weekly in November 1935[19] he used an analogy which he was to deploy to greater effect later: 'Modern man is rather like a bisected wasp which goes on sucking jam and pretends that the loss of its abdomen doesn't matter.' The missing abdomen, its transpires, is man's spiritual being – his soul – nurtured on a belief in the afterlife. Oblivious to the significance of his spiritual deprivation, man continues to gorge himself on sensual gratification, an unedifying and finally self-defeating activity which Orwell finds, in the most literal sense, unfulfilling.

I believe that Crick is mistaken to conclude that all Orwell retained was a pronounced anti-Catholicism and an attachment to the liturgy and traditions of the Church of England.[20] I believe that his thought continued to be shaped by Christianity and that he continued to think it would be inappropriate to admit as much. Intellectuals could gain kudos from declaring a commitment (or better still a conversion) to Marxism, anarchism or even Roman Catholicism – but Anglicanism? It had done little to enhance T. S. Eliot's reputation. True, there is little evidence to suggest that Orwell was over-concerned with what others thought, or that he was generally reluctant for any reason to make his own position known. However, he wrote for a specific audience; he wrote for people like himself, the reflective middle-class concerned with social injustice but not at all impressed with the record in this (or indeed any) field of the established Church. A professed allegiance to Anglicanism would certainly have been a hindrance. More important though, Orwell was temperamentally unsuited to being a regular soldier in anybody's army; he was an irregular fighting in his own way under his own command. His version of Anglicanism would certainly have been individualistic, indeed probably heretical. I have taken some trouble over this point because I believe that Orwell remained deeply committed to the major tenets of Protestant Christianity and, as I have said, I believe that this commitment can be shown to have had a profound effect upon his politics.

In 1932 Orwell received his best Christmas present: advance copies of *Down and Out*. The book was published two weeks later and received, on the whole, favourable reviews from, amomgst others, C. Day Lewis, J. B. Priestley and Compton Mackenzie. Not long after, he had shown the reworked first hundred pages of *Burmese Days* to his agent who was most encouraging. By the end of that year Orwell had moved to a new school, finished the typescript of the new novel, and gone down with pneumonia again. His condition caused such concern this time that Mrs Blair was sent for, though by the time she arrived the crisis was over. But illness did not stop him; with *Burmese Days* still unpublished, primarily because of fears of libel, Orwell began work on *A Clergyman's Daughter* while recuperating with his parents at South-wold. By October of 1934 he had sent his completed typescript to his agent and was already planning his next work, which was to be *Keep the Aspidistra Flying*. By November 1934 Orwell had moved to London, where a job had been found for him in a bookshop.

It was at this stage of his career that Orwell first encountered socialism intellectually; that is to say, he found himself with friends who were socialists and who were able, through discussion, to help him construct an analytical framework for his general criticism of a social structure which seemed to comprise oppressors and oppressed. Orwell became familiar with Marx's major works, and with the arguments and ambitions of mainstream British socialism, but he did not formally become a socialist of any sort. It is nevertheless noteworthy that even before his pilgrimage to the North of England, Orwell was beginning to observe and comment on working-class social and political values,[21] though he did not associate them with socialism as he was later to do.

Meanwhile Orwell's literary career continued to splutter. *A Clergyman's Daughter* had encountered the same libel difficulties as its predecessor, and it was only after great heart-searching that Gollancz decided to go ahead with publication without any major revision, the novel finally appearing in March 1935. It did not receive the critical acclaim of *Burmese Days* (published in New York in October 1934, but not in England until Gollancz took the plunge in June 1935), indeed the author was later to disown it entirely, but it was generally welcomed as exhibiting some fine writing. The publication of *Burmese Days* and its subsequent favourable review by his old prep-school acquaintance Cyril Connolly brought the two men together again and it was at a party hosted by Connolly that Orwell met his future wife Eileen O'Shaughnessy. Eileen's family had come over to England in the nineteenth century and settled in the North East, where Eileen herself was born in 1905. She had an older brother, Laurence, to whom she was devoted. Laurence had trained as a surgeon, and had gone on to be elected to a fellowship of the Royal College of Surgeons at the age of only twenty-six. He had subsequently established a national reputation for research into heart disease and tuberculosis.[22] Eileen was an English graduate of St Hugh's College, Oxford. She had not, however, found herself a satisfying career after graduating, and when she met Orwell she was living with her brother and his wife in Blackheath and studying for an MA in psychology at University College, under Sir Cyril Burt. Eileen was, by disposition if not by formal adoption, a socialist, and her influence tended to cement the developments which had been altering Orwell's perceptions. She was also to influence his writing, being clearly if indirectly responsible for the 'happy ending' of Orwell's next novel, *Keep the Aspidistra Flying*. Like his other novels, this was largely autobiographical, and was finished in January 1936. Eileen was an able and perceptive critic, one of the most intelligent women Orwell knew, and just as widely read as he. Crick feels that she influenced his style,[22] which became more settled, simplified and consistent. This novel was to prove the last of his apprenticeship, the last with no clear and coherent political perspective, and as such marks a watershed in his career.

Having established the development in Orwell's pattern of thinking during the years prior to his departure for the North, it is useful to consider the three early books and the extent to which they mirror or indeed enhance this development. It makes best sense to consider Orwell's books in the order in which they were lived rather than in the order of publication; this way we can follow the sequence of events in his career more easily. *Down and Out in Paris and London* constitutes an autobiographical account of Orwell's experiences in those cities in 1932 and 1933. In this book the author continuously switches from identifying with the poor and writing about society from their point of view to identifying with 'society' and writing about the poor as a social problem. It might be that his original intention was simply to gather material for writing – indeed he states more than once that characters he has met would be suitable subjects for biography – but almost from the beginning his concern focuses on broader social aspects. He becomes a sociologist *à la* Jack London; observing, enumerating, measuring, comparing; and there are no biographies, only thumb-nail sketches. A picture emerges of a writer not quite sure whether he is an observer or a participant. He poignantly observes, for example, that 'a man who has gone even a week on bread and margarine is not a man any longer, only a belly with a few accessory organs',[24] and yet on the previous page, in describing the pitfalls of attempting to survive on six francs a day, he explained how, having spent his last eighty centimes on a litre of milk, he threw it away because a bug had dropped into it while he was boiling it. It is impossible to believe that any of those with whom Orwell lived would have even considered doing the same. Poverty, he says, annihilates the future; apparently it does not annihilate fastidiousness.

Perhaps it is precisely this tension which gives the book its interest, with Orwell trying to 'tell it like it is' but continually, and consciously, telling it like the middle class would imagine it was. Some of the characters that Orwell introduces, especially in the first, Parisian, half of the book, are of intrinsic interest. Boris, for example, an *émigré* White Russian junior officer, is permitted to emerge as a character in his own right but is also used as a kind of exemplar of the aspirations and lifestyle of the under-class from whose ranks come the *plongeurs* of Paris. Similarly, the cameo character of Charlie, who expatiates on the beauty of love, is allowed to tell a story of Huysmanesque debauchery at some length (in a piece of prose so stereotypical as to be almost a pastiche), only for Orwell to conclude almost dismissively : 'He was a curious specimen, Charlie. I describe him just to show what diverse characters could be found flourishing in the Coq d'Or quarter.'[25] One might go as far as to suggest that the book is at its most interesting when Orwell drops his commitment to the detachment of the sociological observer. He tells, for example, of the alleged secret society of 'Communists' who preyed upon Russian *émigrés* by extracting entrance fees from them and then making promises of how the new members' talents would be used, only to disappear subsequently without trace. The society also insisted that new members, on their next visit, should bring bundles of washing because the society was fronting as a laundry. 'Their office looked exactly as a secret Communist office should look, and as for that touch about bringing a parcel of washing, it was genius.' A more imaginative writer, such as Gilbert Chesterton, could have based an entire novel upon this incident.[26]

In fairness to Orwell, however, it is by careful observation that he is able to substantiate his keenest generalisations. Boris, for example, when trying to get work, curses the fact that he *looks* out of a job: 'It is fatal to look hungry. It makes people want to kick you.'[27] Later Orwell managed to find a day's work at a hotel but, being offered a month's work, he rejected it because of a previous promise . He was rounded on by Boris: 'Honest! Honest! Who ever heard of a *plongeur* being honest? . . . Do you think a *plongeur* can afford a sense of honour?'[28] On reflection Orwell recognised the wisdom of this observation and recognised, too, that the hotels themselves act without mercy or scruple towards their employees. More interesting, perhaps, is Orwell's comment on waiters' attitudes. They never despise dinner guests but rather think: ' "One day, when I have saved enough money, I shall be able to imitate that man." He is ministering to a kind of pleasure he thoroughly understands and admires. And that is why waiters are seldom socialists.'[29] Perhaps Orwell has stumbled on something more significant than he imagines; perhaps what Marx referred to as false consciousness is, in some working people, an envy mixed with ambition, a general desire on their part not for a condition of equality but for a hierarchical structure in which they are exploiter rather than exploited. This might explain, to take only one example, why there was little support for the principle of comprehensive education amongst working people in England in the late 1950s and early 1960s: these parents simply wanted their own children to benefit from a grammar school education. Orwell's observations rise naturally from the people and conditions he was describing at first hand. The more he advances into political speculation without this solid support, the less valid his observations become. For example, it is Orwell's view that workers like the *plongeurs* are kept in work which is 'stupid and largely unnecessary' because the rich feel that they would be dangerous if they had more leisure. It is a somewhat precious explanation of the origin and *raison d'être* of good hotels and restaurants and very much at odds with his earlier observations. For all this, the Parisian half of *Down and Out* holds the interest throughout and is clearly enriched by the tension between observation and participation.

Lynette Hunter, in *George Orwell: The Search for a Voice*[30] suggests that Orwell's style mirrors the extent of his involvement. When Orwell has enough to live on in Paris his style reflects the values of what Hunter calls 'the middle-class magazine reader' — very much the detached observer. When he and Boris are hungry and forced to look for work his style becomes more terse and direct. Once he has a job, he becomes more expansive and generalises from his experiences. He has become wiser and has lost many of his middle-class prejudices about the nature of poverty: he wishes to help his middle-class readership experience a similar development. In 1989 a personal, annotated copy of *Down and Out* which Orwell had sent to Brenda Salkeld came to light. Shelden read the author's marginal comments with care. His conclusions put the relationship between style and approach in a different perspective. 'It's the only moment in Orwell's career when we can see the split. As Eric Blair he is saying "George Orwell said this, but I as Eric Blair felt this." He had seized upon a way of creating himself as Orwell, of hiding Blair almost perfectly for the rest of his life. But at the beginning of his writing career, the lines were not so carefully drawn.'[31] In Hunter's terms, 'Blair' can be seen to represent the middle-class magazine reader, 'Orwell' the hungry job-seeker. Shelden is wrong, though, to say that 'Blair' had seized upon a way of creating 'Orwell'. In fact 'Orwell' was painstakingly, indeed painfully, built up over these early years and 'Blair' could have been conscious of what was happening only with the passing of time. 'Orwell' was to become the writer's finest creative achievement and was to transform his prose, but already this fictional character enabled the writer to place himself, as Raymond Williams put it, inside the experiences he was writing about. Eventually 'Orwell' came to represent what Rodden called 'a persona of such style and simplicity . . . the Common Man arguing plain common sense'.[32]

The second half of *Down and Out*, by comparison, is rather dull. Orwell's Parisian companions were from a wide variety of backgrounds; there is not the same diversity amongst his British tramps. Orwell's purpose in the second half seems to have been much more educational. He takes for granted that tramps are generally despised and seen as being the authors of their own misfortune. He seeks to establish the case that the tramp is usually a victim and in no way different from the rest of society. On the other hand, the only character who excited Orwell's admiration, the pavement artist Bozo, had quite a different view. He drew Orwell's attention to Paddy, an 'old moocher' whom he described as only fit to 'scrounge for fag-ends'. That, he said, is the condition in which most tramps finish. But it need not be like that. If a man is educated he can survive, even if he is on the road for life. Orwell disagreed, aguing that when a man has no money he has no ambition, no pride, no self-respect; he is fit for nothing. But Bozo remained adamant that it made no difference, rich or poor: choices remained. 'You just got to say to yourself, ''I'm a free man in *here*'' – he tapped his forehead – and you're alright.'[33] But Bozo was an exceptional character by any standards and, notwithstanding his opinions, Orwell's view of the totally debilitating effects of poverty on the ordinary person remained intact.

Orwell concluded his account by declaring that he would never again think of tramps as scoundrels, nor expect gratitude from a beggar he has tipped, nor be surprised at the lethargy of the unemployed; neither would he subscribe to the Salvation Army, nor pawn his clothes, refuse a handbill or enjoy a meal at a smart restaurant. 'That is a beginning.' And this is exactly what *Down and Out* was to prove: the beginning of a mission in which Orwell would seek to explore, understand and champion the values of the oppressed against their oppressors.

Orwell's next major work was also chiefly autobiographical but in this case a novel, *A Clergyman's Daughter*. It concerns a brief but exciting period in the life of Dorothy Hare, the daughter of the somewhat mean-spirited vicar of a rural East Anglian parish. Dorothy's life seems to be almost unrelentingly dreary, with a wide range of chores, domestic and social, including the running of her father's vicarage – he was a widower – on a shoe-string. She has little time to consider her faith, in fact little time for any spiritual preoccupations, though she is continually being sustained by natural beauty, as when, for example, a 'momentary spear of sunlight' catches a spray of leaves in the church doorway, turning them as green as the waters of the Atlantic. That flash of colour gave Dorothy back 'by a process deeper than reason, her peace of mind, her love of God, her power of worship'.[34] Later in the book, the scent of a frond of fennel, pressed against her cheek produces a similar effect, swelling her heart with a mystical joy which she recognised, perhaps mistakenly, she concedes, as the love of God.[35] Dorothy's joy directly reflects Orwell's own great love of natural beauty and for him, too, it had an almost mystical dimension.

The novel deals at some length with the more wordly side of religious life, the internecine strife within the Anglican community, between, on the one hand, the High Churchers and the Low Churchers, and on the other the High Churchers and the Anglo-Catholics. It becomes clear that at this stage of his life these battles, whose detritus littered the pages of the *Church Times*, were important to Orwell. Dorothy's life is complicated by the attentions of Warburton, a middle-aged man who enjoys a bad reputation and who makes intermittent and surprisingly clumsy attempts to seduce her. One such attempt, made when she was at a particularly low ebb physically and emotionally, was enough to cause Dorothy to become aphasic, to lose her memory and to leave home.

This sudden twist of fate allows the author to whisk his character off on just the kind of excursion which he himself was apt to make. She travels down to Kent in the company of some down-and-outs, to pick hops. The events described are very largely based upon Orwell's own experiences as set out in his essays, and he uses them principally to depict the horrific conditions in which many of the poor lived and also to show how innate human decency could rise above such squalor. Towards the end of the hop-picking season Dorothy's memory begins to return and she writes to her father. Unfortunately, her sudden departure had provided an excellent opportunity for some imaginative journalism in the press and she has been pictured as having led a life of carnal abandon with her lover Warburton; as a consequence, her father is not too keen to have her back. He has made provision for a relative to help her but she, not having received his correspondence and thus being unaware of his

plans, has to live rough in London awaiting – she did not know what. Her
stay in London, however, provides the opportunity for the author to
switch to Joycean dramatic dialogue for thirty pages. This intermission
does little for the development of the plot and less for the literary
reputation of the author. Eventually Dorothy is rescued from squalor,
poverty and literary experimentation by the man-servant of a relation of
her father's who, at his request, had found her a post in a small private
school in west London. Once again, Orwell's inspiration draws upon his
own experiences. Her life as a teacher resembles Orwell's own teaching
days mixed with a flavour of St Cyprian's. Dorothy is given sound advice
by her employer, Mrs Creevy, to punish only those girls whose parents
were bad payers, but she had little advice on the curriculum. Dorothy's
attempts to liberalise the teaching programme come to an abrupt end
after parents began to complain following Dorothy's attempted explanation to her class of what Shakespeare had meant by describing MacDuff as
having been 'from his mother's womb untimely ripped'. Eventually
Dorothy is dimissed from her post, not as result of any dereliction of
duty, or indeed unduly liberal teaching techniques, but simply because
Mrs Creevy herself had been made a better financial proposition. At this
point Warburton arrives with the news that all had been forgiven at
home and that he is to take her back immediately.

So life for Dorothy turns full circle, with Warburton – no *deus ex
machina* – unsuccessfully forcing his attentions upon her and offering
marriage on the train journey, and her former lifestyle and duties, like an
old winter coat behind the kitchen door of the vicarage, waiting to be put
on again. What has changed? Dorothy has lost her faith. Or so she says.
Are we to assume that this, too, is autobiographical? I think it very likely
is, and so is worth considering with some care. While still teaching,
Dorothy discovered that she had lost the power of worship. Yet this loss
did not deter her from attending church; quite the reverse – her
attendances became 'blessed interludes of peace'. Dorothy perceived
that for all the worldliness and stupidity of church politics, there
remained something 'of decency, of spiritual comeliness – that is not
easy to find in the outside world'. It was better to go to church than not,
'better to follow the ancient ways, than drift in rootless freedom'.[36]
Later, when she discusses her loss of faith with Warburton, she argues
that pretending to believe is the next best thing to believing, for she
'recoiled from a world discovered to be meaningless'. Warburton the
free thinker told her that she was trying to have the worst of both worlds,

sticking to a Christian regimen but without the promise of eternal life. No doubt, he concluded, there were many in her position – Anglican atheists – 'wandering about among the ruins of the C of E'.

Dorothy concludes that despite the loss of her faith she has not changed and did not wish to change 'the spiritual background of her mind . . . her cosmos . . . was still in a sense the Christian cosmos . . . the Christian life was still the way that must come natural to her'.[37] Later she reflects on the arguments for God's existence, recognising that the problem had no solution. There was, she understood, no viable substitute for faith; 'no pagan acceptance of life as sufficient to itself, no pantheistic cheer-up stuff, no pseudo-religion of 'progress' with visions of glittering Utopias . . . Either life on earth is a preparation for something greater and more lasting, or it is meaningless, dark and dreadful.'[38] The latter prospect frightened her. She had discovered the 'deadly emptiness at the heart of things'. Dorothy buckled down to living the life of a Christian.

What are we to make of this dissection of Dorothy's soul, in the light of Orwell's own spiritual development? We can assume that, like Dorothy, he found it impossible to slough off his Anglican frame of mind and that, while he had lost faith in the certainty of eternal life, he never felt intellectually able to dismiss the possibility. More importantly, Christianity, especially Anglicanism, represented a way of life infinitely superior to any 'life-for-its-own-sake' philosophy. If what Orwell says about Dorothy reflects his own thinking, then he is not accurately described by the phrase 'Anglican atheist'. Moreover, it is important to recognise that, if Dorothy is any guide, politics belongs to the Christian cosmos, and that Christian values, in politics as in all things, are preferable to any other, irrespective of whether life was a preparation for something greater and more lasting or something meaningless, dark and dreadful. Finally, as has been pointed out, the resolution of the plot seems to suggest an acceptance of the 'inequalities and iniquities of social life that it must be said, deny the liberal, much less the radical spirit'.[39] Dorothy comes back to the cardboard armour and the glue pot. 'If one gets on into the job that lies to hand the ultimate purpose of the job fades into insignificance.'[40] In most respects, then, it can be said that Dorothy chooses God and not man, a matter that will give cause for some discussion later on.

The third and final novel to be considered here is *Keep the Aspidistra Flying*. Again basically autobiographical, the novel covers the period of

Orwell's life when he was working in the bookshop and beginning to make his way in the literary world. The central character, Gordon Comstock, is an aspiring poet who has forsaken a 'good' job with an advertising agency not merely because he want to concentrate upon his writing, but because he has no wish to succeed in what nowadays would be called the rat race. Gordon feels his desertion from the 'real world' very keenly, only too aware of the sacrifices made by his family to get him settled in life. To make matters worse he hates his new bohemian lifestyle and especially his lack of money. Indeed the book is very largely about money, or more accurately, the lack of it: in fact, Orwell had originally wanted to call the novel *In Praise of Poverty*. It begins with an adaptation of 1 Corinthians xiii which concludes: 'And now abideth faith, hope and money, these three; but the greatest of these is money'. Like the hero of Gissing's *New Grub Street*, to which the novel is indebted, Comstock's reaction to poverty is not that of the naturally poor but that of a man whose previous lifestyle and experience lead him to a set of expectations which the ordinary poor do not have, and which he cannot realise. What makes poverty harder for Comstock to accept is that it is self-imposed; the advertising agency would always give him his job back if he were to ask. This is an important point to grasp because Orwell uses Comstock in an emblematic manner: poverty constrains the lives of the under-privileged in so many ways; nobody without money in their pocket can be considered, or indeed considers themselves, a complete person. It is lack of money that alienates, possession of money that makes a person whole – hence the reference to Corinthians. But in reality Comstock is no emblem of the disadvantaged, and if he represents Orwell's level of understanding of and sympathy for the poor at this stage of his life, then the journey to the North which he was soon to make wrought a most dramatic transformation.

Comstock is consumed in almost equal measure by self-pity and abhorrence of wealth. Looking at an effeminate young man as he left the bookshop Comstock remarks: 'The skin at the back of his neck was silky-smooth as the inside of a shell. You can't have a skin like that for under five hundred a year.'[41] In conversation with his well-to-do friend Ravelston (an unflattering portrait of Richard Rees) Comstock later argues: 'Don't you see that a man's whole personality is bound up with his income? His personality *is* his income. How can you be attractive to a girl when you've got no money?' It is the assumed link with sexual attraction which clearly establishes the importance of money for Comstock, for in truth it is women and not men who worship the money-god: 'A woman's got a sort of mystical feeling towards money. Good and evil in a woman's mind simply mean money and no money.'[42] What Comstock means by this is that most women seek financial security before everything and their task is to make men conform in order to achieve that security. Comstock's fiancée Rosemary passionately wished to rescue him from what he very unpoetically refers to as 'the abyss where poetry is written', to reinstall him in his former job and to set up home with him and have a family. This, for Comstock would represent final defeat; it was no coincidence that Rosemary's surname is Waterlow. Final defeat would mean 'selling your soul for a villa and an aspidistra . . . what a fate!'

Are there no alternatives to either poverty or a suburban villa complete with aspidistra? Ravelston tried to convince Comstock that socialism offered an alternative; a social and political system which would eliminate poverty and the dominance of money and replace them with an efficient, progressive, equal and caring society. Comstock remained far from convinced and characterised socialism as four hours spent in a pleasant factory tightening bolt number 6003, followed by rations served communally out of grease-proof paper and then a community hike from Marx hostel to Lenin hostel and back. While Orwell is aware that this description of socialism is a travesty it is clear that he did indeed link socialism with planning and mechanisation, and thus see it in part at least as the enemy not the friend of the poor. Comstock sees socialism as one of three alternatives 'and all three of them make us spew' – the other two were suicide and the Roman Catholic church. And already Orwell was beginning to see that socialism as a system – that is, imposed from above by Ravelston and his fellow intellectuals – with its belief in planning, would be as inimical to working-class values as capitalism. 'How right the lower classes are. Hats off to the factory lad who with fourpence in the world puts his girl in the family way! At least he's got blood and not money in his veins.'[44] Neither has he planning in his veins; for better or worse he is his own man, not to be dominated by 'systems'. He will become, in Orwell's last book, the repository of mankind's last hope against totalitarianism.

It is Comstock's abhorrence of planning which brings about his own downfall (or salvation), for Rosemary becomes pregnant and they marry – no alternative for Comstock as abortion is unthinkable. His response to that option indicates Orwell's essentially spiritual attitude to life. Comstock recognises that what they were discussing was no mere abstration but flesh and blood, not a concept but life, a 'bit of himself' which was alive within her. This realisation drew them closer together than ever before. They experienced a strange sympathy such as they had never had before. 'For a moment he did feel that in some mysterious way they were one flesh . . . He knew that it was a dreadful thing they were contemplating – a blasphemy.' There was nothing for it but to buy that villa and put an aspidistra, symbol of middle-class stability and respectability, in the window. When it was done Comstock felt only relief at the prospect of what he acknowledged to be a decent life. And in any case, he was merely fulfilling his destiny. 'In some corner of his mind he had always known that this would happen.'[45] Nothing emblematic here; there is no comparable Waterloo available to the poor and since Comstock is seen to be following his fate when he rejoins the advertising agency and takes up his role in bourgeois society, we understand that finally his action has no specifically political implication, but a moral one: Comstock is taking up the cardboard armour and the glue pot. Elsewhere Orwell wrote discerningly that the essence of being human is that one does not seek perfection, that 'one does not push asceticism to the point where it makes friendly intercourse impossible, and that one is prepared in the end to be defeated and broken up for life, which is the inevitable price of fastening one's love upon other human individuals'.[46] No doubt the untypically 'happy' ending owes more to the influence of Orwell's own partner, Eileen O'Shaughnessy, than it does to any development in his political ideology or moral philosophy.

The themes of both *The Clergyman's Daughter* and *Keep The Aspidistra Flying* are similar: disenchantment, escape, failure and reintegration; and belong more securely in the nineteenth-century novel than that of the twentieth. Perhaps, as Raymond Williams suggests, Orwell saw his own career in these terms. Reintegration always implies defeat for Orwell's characters. There was still considerable disagreement at this time regarding Orwell's skills as a creative writer. Q. D. Leavis, writing in 1940, was damning:

> Mr Orwell must have wasted a lot of energy trying to be a novelist. I think I must have read three or four novels by him and the only impression these dreary books left on me was that nature didn't intend him to be a novelist.[47]

Compton Mckenzie, on the other hand, felt that 'no realistic writer during the last five years has produced three volumes which can compare in directness, vigour, courage and vitality'.[48] From a socialist point of view, however, Raymond Williams is convinced that Orwell's creative powers were not up to the job: he recognises both an artistic and a political shortcoming in Orwell's work. He had not the necessary grasp of socialist ideology to conceive of a form of society in which his characters could integrate without having to admit failure, and neither had he the artistic ability to create such a society even in microcosm.[49] Williams' criticism seems justified on both counts, at least at this stage of Orwell's career. He had not thought his political prejudices through to any coherent ideological position and his creative writing was limited as a consequence. George Woodcock perceptively criticised these novels as lacking stylistic and structural homogeneity. They are, he continues, spoilt by 'self-conscious theorising and social commentary which however well they may suit Orwell's autobiographical works merely disfigure his fiction'.[50] In short, Orwell the creative writer was waiting for the emergence of Orwell the socialist.

3 The politics of decency

In January 1936 the publisher Victor Gollancz took a decision which was to have considerable consequences for modern political writing and arguably for modern politics in Britain: he commissioned Orwell to write a book about the condition of the life of the unemployed in the North of England. Orwell accepted the commission eagerly, since it involved an advance of £500, representing approximately two years of his living expenses. This commission represented a measure of success for Orwell, being both a recognition that he was a writer to be reckoned with and an indicator of a more stable and certain financial future. He was able to get married, after having first explained to Eileen that she should expect to live in a working class lifestyle. The gist of Gollancz's reasoning was that Orwell had shown, in *Down and Out*, the ability to write with insight about the lives of the poor: why not give a more political focus to his writing by commissioning him to undertake a similar task with regard to the Northern working class?.

Having resigned from the bookshop, Orwell set out for the North as soon as he could, towards the end of January. He was to visit Wigan, Barnsley and Sheffield over the next two months, though also spending a little time with his sister and family in Leeds. Orwell's talents for the task in hand were extraordinarily apt: he was a journalist and a novelist but also had considerable experience of living in poverty. He had the trained mind of the observer but an instinctive empathy with the subjects of his study. His whole attitude to the task in hand is shown by the method he chose of travelling north. He took the train to Coventry and then made his way up to Manchester on foot and by bus, through the Black Country and up through Staffordshire to Cheshire, staying in cheap hotels and lodging houses. For a Southerner with only limited experience of the North, the Black Country and the Potteries in late January must have been a chastening experience. In Manchester, Orwell sought advice on his trip from Independent Labour Party (ILP) friends of Richard Rees and was recommended to make his way to

Wigan, where ailing mining and textiles industries had brought short-time work and unemployment to many. Furnished with names and addresses Orwell sought lodgings in Wigan. After less than a week he changed his original lodgings, somewhat to the consternation of those who were helping him, because of their cleanliness and good order; this was not what he had come to experience. Crick quotes one worker who tried to help Orwell as complaining: 'He could have gone to any of a thousand respectable working-class houses . . . but he doesn't do that. He goes straight to a doss-house, just like he's down and out in Paris still.'[1]

Orwell soon established himself above a tripe shop generally considered to be a 'right filthy hole'[2] and stayed for two weeks. He used his lodgings as no more than a backdrop in his writing and spent most of his time visiting people's houses and gleaning statistics from the local library on living and working conditions. In Yorkshire, too, Orwell was to collect statistics, cull newspaper reports and meet many working-class people, especially miners, most of whom were either socialists or communists. Those who met Orwell, Lancastrians and Yorkshiremen, and who subsequently wrote about him, seem agreed that he was not a socialist in any formal sense but that he had an instinctive sympathy for the poor. They agreed, too, that he took considerable pains to understand the background to the way the Means Test operated and to assess the effect that it was having on the lives of the unemployed. But none of them really seemed to understand what he was up to.

Of all the experiences about which he wrote none affected Orwell more than his three trips down coal mines. One man who accompanied Orwell later recounted on a BBC programme that having knocked himself out on a girder Orwell had to crawl three quarters of a mile bent double to arrive at a workface only 26 inches high. He was utterly exhausted though he recovered sufficiently to have a drink with his companions immediately afterwards. His trips down the mines had an indelible effect upon this man whose physique could hardly have been less suited to coal mining. For the middle-class Southerner it might have been an experience of life on another planet.[3]

This first trip brought on a bout of bronchitis which Orwell suffered while visiting Liverpool and staying with more friends of Richard Rees. It was his good fortune to find a warm and comfortable bed with people who were willing to care for him so that within a few days he was able to visit the docks and watch the taking on of men in the morning, an undignified and often squalid process in the days of casual labour. Shortly afterwards, Orwell returned to Wigan and then, having seen what he had wanted to see and having met most of those he had been advised to speak to, he decided to cross the Pennines to Yorkshire. In the bank, so to speak, he had salted away what he had come for; the bones of an account *à la* Jack London of the lives of the poor amply supported by statistical information and first-hand experience. But he had also accrued an unexpected bonus: he had witnessed working-class socialists trying to make ideological sense of the economic chaos of which they were a reluctant part, and this had brought socialism to life for him in a way which the texts he read in London failed to do. Moreover, he had witnessed a pattern of living among the poor which was to affect him even more greatly than it had Siegfried Sassoon when he had experienced it in the trenches of Flanders. Orwell called it decency. His experiences in Yorkshire would only replicate and so reinforce the lessons of Wigan and Liverpool.

Orwell's first stop was Sheffield, where he arrived in early March. He stayed in a miner's back-to-back house and was given an exhaustive three days of visits and meetings. The people to whom Orwell spoke were nearly always a small self-selected group of politically conscious left-wing workers. Orwell was aware of this fact, but it did not prevent him missing the main political expressions of ordinary working-class values, the trade union movement and the Labour party. Later Orwell wrote, often quite trenchantly, about both, but it must be said that, unlike his comments on working-class life at the family or community level, his comments on working class political values as expressed by the unions or the Labour party were not the product of detailed observation.

After Sheffield Orwell sought respite with his sister and brother-in-law in Leeds for a week, and then came on to Barnsley, where he was to stay for two weeks. He made two further trips down mines, at Wentworth Woodhouse (which D. H. Lawrence had visited) and Grimethorpe Colliery. It was while he was in Barnsley that Orwell went to a public meeting to hear Oswald Mosley speak, and the Marxists he was with were ejected for asking too robust questions of the speaker. One of them told of an argument later in which Orwell had claimed that Mosley should have been allowed to speak and be rebutted only by argument. The Marxists thought him dangerously naive;

indeed Orwell himself was deeply concerned at how easy it had been for Mosley to bamboozle an uneducated audience.

At the end of March Orwell left south Yorkshire for the 'languorous South' for which he had begun to pine,[4] and was never to travel to the 'barbaric regions' of the North again. He had gathered his information and had now the task of organizing the material for publication. Fortunately this was made easier by the fact that some of his friends had found a home for the Orwells, an old cottage in the Hertfordshire village of Wallington. Orwell lived there for four years. It was by no means picturesque, having no bathroom and no inside toilet, but it had an ample garden in which Orwell grew vegetables and kept chickens and goats. In May of 1936, just a few weeks after the publication of *Keep the Aspidistra Flying*, Orwell began work on *Wigan Pier*. He was briefly distracted in June by preparations for his wedding, the service being conducted in a local church according to the marriage rites of the Church of England. Crick passes this off as an idiosyncrasy, consented to primarily for family reasons. However, Orwell clearly took the matter seriously, spending time studying the Prayer Book beforehand,[5] a quite unnecessary chore for anyone going through the motions. Once again we see the paradoxical relationship between the public and the private man regarding religion.

During the summer of 1936 events of great consequence were unfolding in Spain. A democractically elected left-wing government had abolished the monarchy and stripped the church of much of its power. The Spanish military, led by General Franco, had rebelled and marched on Madrid. To considerable surprise Franco's Moorish troops were repulsed and further to the north, in Catalonia, a government even more radical than the Madrid government took power in the name of the workers. These events prompted socialists and communists throughout western Europe to support the republicans in a variety of ways, chiefly by forming the International Brigade. Many in Britain decided to join the fight, seeing it as the first skirmish in the coming war against the totalitarian regimes, whose support for Franco was overt and considerable. Orwell, too, decided to go, though he made sure to finish *Wigan Pier* first. By December he was able to send off the completed manuscript, feeling satisfied that he had come close to saying what *he* wanted, but knowing that it would not prove to be what Gollancz wanted. He was right, and Gollancz tried to get Orwell to agree to the initial publication of both halves of the book separately, with the first half being published later under the imprimatur of the Left Book Club. Orwell would have none of this, and eventually Gollancz was obliged to publish the whole, though in an introduction he was careful to make his own position clear, warmly praising Orwell's descriptions of working-class life in the first half of the book but being broadly critical of his stance in the second in which he attacked socialist intellectuals. The book was published in March 1937, while Orwell was in the front line in Spain, and proved a substantial if controversial success.

In his introduction to the Left Book Club edition, Gollancz criticised the author for advocating 'emotional socialism' in the second part of the book, having clearly established in the first half problems of such severity that could only be solved by 'scientific socialism'. Others were to be more critical. Raymond Williams unfairly asserted that Orwell had painted class differences as being basically about accent, and then had sold this line to his middle-class readers.[6] Laski probably spoke for most socialist intellectuals when he wrote in a similar vein that *Wigan Pier*

> ignores all that is implied in the urgent reality of class antagonisms. [Orwell] refuses to confront the grave problem of the State. He has no sense of the historic movement of the economic process. At bottom, in fact, it is an emotional plea for socialism addressed to comfortable people.[7]

Orwell would probably not have objected to that charge because in some respects at least that was precisely what the book was meant to be. Much later Toynbee wrote that *Wigan Pier* 'reads like a report brought back by some humane anthropologist who has just returned from studying the conditions of an oppressed tribe in Borneo'.[8] Even this, given the amount of ignorance – in which Orwell himself had shared – about living and working conditons in the North, is not wide of the mark. Orwell would have been less pleased with the reaction of the Northern working-class novelist Walter Greenwood, whom the book infuriated – though it held his attention.[9] As for the author himself, it is difficult to overemphasise the book's importance in his own development as a writer; in Rees's words the researching and writing of *Wigan Pier* transformed a smouldering fire into a flame.

Orwell set out for Spain at the end of December. He had first sought some contacts from British communist leaders who, rightly doubting his political reliability (from their point of view), had been disinclined to help. Contacts with the Independent Labour Party, however, had given him a letter of recommendation to their colleagues in Barcelona and with this he set out. On the way through France Orwell paid a visit to the American writer Henry Miller who, appalled at his intentions, tried unsuccessfully to dissuade him. Having reached Barcelona Orwell's letter of recommendation introduced him to John McNair, who put him in contact with the group with which the ILP felt the closest affinity, the Partido Obrero de Unification Marxista (POUM), which was the smallest of the organisations comprising the republican force in Catalonia. The POUM militia was said to be the most politically conscious of the militias and was regarded by its communist ally as being Trotskyist, which was true in part though it was also home for a number of anarchists. It was, in short, a left-wing socialist group. Orwell's prime objective in going to Spain, he admitted, was to fight against the fascists. In fact with his military training at Eton and more importantly in the Imperial Police, he was able to play an important role in helping to train the raw volunteers.

Orwell was to gain a great respect for the Spanish working class, and likewise those among them who got to know him held him in the highest regard. To exercise some sort of unofficial leadership in a militia in which the emphasis was on persuasion rather than orders suited him admirably, and he had few qualms when they moved to the Aragon front at Alcubierre. Towards the end of January he was moved near to Saragossa, where he joined the ILP contingent of about 30 which had just arrived from Britain. Orwell was in the trenches for over three months, seeing action on many occasions, before obtaining leave in Barcelona, where Eileen was staying. The leave was not to be a restful one, however, for after a few days of illness, Orwell witnessed an outbreak of fierce internecine fighting between the anarchists and POUM on the one hand and the communists on the other. He was pleased to get back to the front at Huesca, where at least one knew who and where the enemy was. Ten days later, in mid-May, Orwell was shot through the throat by a sniper. Although seriously wounded he was fortunate; had the bullet struck marginally to the left it would have severed the carotid artery and certainly killed him. Moreover, the wound was a clean one. It was while Orwell was waiting for his discharge that the communist-dominated police began to disarm and arrest POUM and anarchist soldiers and supporters. Eileen, waiting for her husband, had her room searched by police looking for incriminating papers: he was in real danger. He slept rough for several nights and walked the streets in the daytime in an effort to avoid arrest. Meanwhile Eileen got the necessary papers together for their departure and eventually, after a number of alarms, they caught the train for France, braving it out in the restaurant car like tourists. Several of Orwell's friends were far less lucky and suffered imprisonment and death at the hands of the communists and their allies.

The Orwells actually visited one friend, Georges Kopp, held in a Barcelona prison, in an effort to secure his release. Although to no avail this was an act of great courage. Shelden inclines to the view that Eileen had probably had an affair with Kopp a little earlier.[10] If so it is not impossible that Orwell himself would have known. Shelden refers to a security police document from this period which came to light in 1989 in the Madrid National Historical Archive, which proves the extent of the danger the Orwells had been in. They were described in the document as 'known Troskyists' and 'likely agents of the ILP and POUM'. These were certainly grounds for arrest and perhaps much worse.[11]

By the beginning of July the Orwells were back in Wallington, and almost immediately Orwell began work on *Homage to Catalonia*. His experiences in Spain had been formative in a number of ways but principally he came to the view that the truly revolutionary forces on the left were the anarchists and Trotkyists and that the communists and the middle-class supporters of the republic were more concerned to defeat the revolution than they were to defeat Franco. The western powers, too, he believed, were more concerned to prevent revolution in their own countries than to prevent fascism. Orwell had written an article for *The New Statesman and Nation* along these lines but it had been rejected; instead he was offered a review copy of Borkenau's civil war classic *The Spanish Cockpit*. However, the editor, Kingsley Martin, refused to publish even this review when it appeared, and concluded his covering letter by pointing out that although *The New Statesman* relished controversy in its correspondence columns it was not prepared to publish a review that controverted the 'political policy of the paper[12].' He was, nevertheless, prepared to pay Orwell in the normal manner. It requires little imagination to picture how Orwell would have received such a letter.[13]

Back in Hertfordshire Orwell might have been free from stray sniper bullets but he was very soon to find himself subjected to a different form of attack. As we have seen, the second half of *Wigan Pier* had been received with general disfavour by many on the left, especially the communists.[14] Orwell believed that this criticism was largely a consequence of his having fought with POUM and was an attempt to discredit him. In what he wrote about the May fighting in Barcelona, Orwell had declared himself to be an enemy of the communists and clearly, in Britain at least, he was an important one who could best be silenced by being discredited.

Constant criticism steeled Orwell to finish his book about Spain as soon as possible: indeed *Homage to Catalonia* was finished by January of 1938. His political education had been short and sharp and he had come to believe that far from being the enemy of fascism, communism was in effect its ally and, by extension, so were intellectual fellow-travellers, including many of the British left.[15] Fascism could only be opposed by the overthrow of capitalism and not by wars against fascist states; this would only permit fascism entry into capitalist democracies by the back door. Cyril Connolly referred to Orwell at this time as a 'sort of John the Baptist figure coming in from the wilderness' capable of producing an almost magical effect upon those he met.[16] Connolly was referring to a particular incident but his description was generally apt. His long apprenticeship finally complete, Orwell had acquired a political persona and his message for the middle class, like John's, was a message of repentance and of sacrifice. As Koestler said: 'He was merciless towards himself, severe upon his friends, unresponsive to admirers, but full of understanding sympathy for those on the remote periphery.' No wonder Rodden called him a saint.[17] Moreover, Orwell patently attempted to live by the values he preached and, what is more, he had perfected a prose style which enabled him to preach the values he lived.

Crick describes Orwell's status as a writer at this time as 'well-known but not famous' and remarks that he had to remain productive not merely for psychological reassurance but also out of economic necessity. Nevertheless 1938 began inauspiciously. In early March he began to haemorrhage badly and, on the advice of Laurence O'Shaughnessy, went into a sanatorium in Kent. This misfortune put paid to a potential development in Orwell's career which would have changed his future. He had been offered a job with a weekly 'reformist' journal in India as assistant editor and leader writer. He accepted the job, though he made his political allegiances plain to his putative employers, describing himself as 'of socialist sympathies . . . associated to some extent with the ILP'.[18] However, he did not mention his recurring ill-health nor his 'down-and-outing'. The India Office was not keen on the appointment, though it seems unlikely that it would have attempted to prevent his going had the editor been willing to stick to his guns. In the event Orwell pre-empted any tussle by declining the offer on medical advice.

Orwell's attack was a bad one; moving him even by ambulance – a 'very luxurious bedroom on wheels' – was a risk. He remained in the sanatorium for six months and although he was allowed to make trips out into the surrounding countryside he was not to do any writing beyond the odd article. All the same, by the time he left he had worked out the structure for his next novel, *Coming Up For Air*. Orwell used the time not merely for rest and recuperation, which were sorely needed, but also to benefit intellectually from reading, and from conversation and correspondence with the steady stream of visitors which included friends, writers, old comrades and admirers.

Homage to Catalonia was published on April 25th, on the whole to not very favourable reviews. Communists and fellow-travellers quite naturally regarded the work as Trotskyite and anarchist and by definition therefore unsound in a literary as well as a political sense, and none was to give it praise as a piece of political writing. What would no doubt have pleased Orwell greatly, however, was the letter he received from Franz Borkenau. (It had been Orwell's review of his book on Spain which *The New Statesman* had refused to publish.) 'To me,' wrote Borkenau, 'your book is a further confirmation of my conviction that it is possible to be perfectly honest . . . irrespective of one's political convictions.'[19] The book sold very badly – only 700 copies of an unambitious printing of 1,500. Indeed the publisher still had surplus copies as late as 1951.[20] Perhaps it was the debate over his book and his own reflections while on 'extended leave' that finally decided Orwell actually to join the ILP, which he did in June, explaining his reasons in an article in *The New Leader* on June 24th. 'It is vitally necessary,' he wrote, 'that there should be in existence some body of people who can be depended on, even in the face of persecution, not to compromise their socialist principles.'[21] Interestingly, in the light of his later scathing attacks on pacifism, Orwell had also joined the Peace Pledge Union in late 1937, and had written an anti-war pamphlet which he could not get published and of which, surprisingly, no copy appears to exist.[22]

During these months, Orwell was also turning his mind to analysing the nature of totalitarianism. What concerned him was that human nature might not be a constant. Whereas in the past it had been a fundamental belief in the value of liberty (which Orwell clearly took to be synonymous with human nature) which had eventually brought down even the Inquisition, perhaps totalitarian systems, with their hegemonic control of all socialising agencies, might produce citizens who did not desire liberty.[23] More arresting from the point of view of his later thinking is that Orwell read and reviewed, in the summer of 1938, Eugene Lyons' *Assignment in Utopia*. He presciently remarked: 'It is an unfortunate fact that any hostile criticism of the present Russian regime is liable to be taken as propaganda *against socialism*; all socialists are aware of this . . . .'[24] He also concluded that the Soviet system which Lyons described was not very different from fascism, with its hero-worship, totalitarian social control, induced mass-hatred and show trials.[25]

On the health front progress was considerable and in July he was allowed to have the use of his typewriter again. However, there was a fear that his customary attack of winter bronchitis might reopen the lesion and he was advised to winter abroad. Although this would not have been possible for financial reasons, a friend and admirer put up the money and so, in early September, after a week spent at Southwold Orwell and his wife left for north Africa. They rented a small villa near Marrakesh, acquired a goat and some hens, planted some vegetables and settled for six months. Orwell had mapped out his next novel. Morocco was not a search for new experiences but simply a retreat in which he could write. His health was not particularly good, though perhaps it would have been far worse had he stayed in Britain. In fact both he and Eileen were ill during this period and their marriage appears to have come under considerable strain. As Orwell became more obsessed with the bleakness of the future so Eileen found him more wearing, indeed exasperating.[26] Nevertheless when he and Eileen got back to London in early April of 1939, shortly after the collapse of the Spanish republic, Orwell was able to deliver the manuscript of *Coming Up For Air* to Victor Gollancz. They then made their way back to Wallington.

Although it must have been a considerable relief to get back to the chores of their country life (a neighbour and fellow left-wing writer Jack Common had taken care of the place during their absence), nobody, least of all Orwell, could have believed that they were coming back to a normal life: war straddled the horizon. Orwell had a visit from the local police, who impounded some of his books – those from the French Obelisk Press who had published Henry Miller. The Public

Prosecutor later wrote to Orwell accepting that a writer 'might have a need for books which it was illegal to possess'. However the incident could only have fuelled Orwell's fears.[27]

Nevertheless, in May Orwell began work on a series of essays which he was to call *Inside the Whale*. In early June *Coming Up For Air* appeared, to generally favourable reviews; it was to sell out within a couple of years. Only a few days after this triumph his father died and Orwell made the journey to Southwold. Nobody who has written on Orwell has claimed that there was much affection between father and son, but the formal relationship, at least, remained and was reinforced by mutual respect. When all is said and done, of course, they had little in common, but all the same, Mr Blair took pleasure in his son's success; indeed according to Orwell his father's last conscious moments were spent listening to a very favourable *Sunday Times* review of *Coming Up For Air*; this must have been a considerable comfort to both men.[28]

In the following month *The Adelphi* published Orwell's last anti-war polemic 'Not Counting Niggers' in which he attacked the motley opponents of fascism in their new unlikely guises – Quakers demanding a bigger army, Churchill posing as a democrat, for example. What he really objected to, he said, was the British and French empires posing as democracies when they were actually simply exploiters of cheap labour who ruled over 'six hundred million disenfranchised human beings'. It was a restatement of his ILP position: fascism simply could not be fought against by a subtler form of fascism. He looked without much hope for the formation of a mass party which would throw off the role of fascism.[29] Within two months Orwell would forsake his anti-war sentiments: at the end of August news broke of the Nazi-Soviet pact. It became immediately apparent that war had become inevitable; Hitler had *carte blanche* to invade Poland, and Britain and France were pledged to support that nation.

It is necessary now to retrace our steps over these crucial years and to look in more detail at Orwell's major writings in order to understand more fully the developments outlined above. The obvious point of departure is of course *Wigan Pier*, a controversial book even by Orwell's standards. The first half of the book is largely descriptive. 'The first sound in the mornings was the clumping of the mill-girls' clogs down the cobbled streets.' This opening sentence lulls us into a false sense of security and only one sentence later we are into a different world, with four men in the one room 'and a beastly place it was'. There follows a lengthy description of the Brookers' house and lifestyle concentrating on the dirt and squalor which Orwell attributes not so much to poverty as to sloth. He captures the habits of the Brookers with merciless accuracy: their meanness of spirit, their self-pity, their life amounting to an 'endless muddle of slovened jobs', but above all their Pinteresque habit of saying the same thing over and over. The comments made by a Cockney travelling salesman, who divined that Orwell was a fellow-Southerner, clearly echo the author's sentiments: 'The filthy bloody bastards!' Nobody who claims that Orwell idealised the working class can have reflected on these pages.

The landscape of industrial Lancashire, as depicted by Orwell, is as unremittingly squalid as the Brookers' house. It provides a backdrop for misery, as witness his well-known description of the woman kneeling to unblock a drain. Although he saw her from the window of a slow-moving train, our observant commentator informs us that the woman, though she looked forty, thanks to miscarriages and drudgery is actually only twenty-five. This poetic license has a reason, for Orwell wishes to attack what he takes to be a popular fallacy, that people brought up in slums can conceive of nothing better and therefore wish for nothing better. This was one of the messages conveyed by Victorian writers like George Gissing in works such as *Demos* and *The Nether World*.

Orwell believed this argument to be nonsensical. 'She knew well enough what was happening to her — understood as well as I did how dreadful a destiny it was to be kneeling there in the bitter cold, on the slimy stones of a slum backyard, poking a stick up a foul drain-pipe.' Yet at the same time this satanic black and grey world provided a backdrop for a kind of resolute heroism made the more heroic because it is on the backs of those who inhabit this world that the rest of us are able to live our lives of comparative cosiness. Standing as the symbol of this class is the miner whom Orwell describes as a kind of 'grimy caryatid upon whose shoulders nearly everything that is *not* grimy is supported'. Orwell puts to good use his trips down the mines to give a chilling description of work underground, and he makes it quite clear that the experience had not merely exhausted him physically but had left him with a most profound respect for those who are obliged to do this work day after day; work which, he readily acknowledged, would have killed him within weeks. Yet whatever the world got up to, from playing test matches to invading Abyssinia, it required men to do this work. 'You and I and the editor of the *Times Lit. Supp.* and the Nancy poets and the

Archbishop of Canterbury and Comrade X, author of *Marxism for Infants* — all of us *really* owe the comparative decency of our lives to poor drudges underground . . . .' Orwell suggests that the relationship is not symbiotic but perhaps parasitic; at the very least he demands that 'we' reassess that relationship, acknowledging the key role of the miner, who stands here as representative of the working class. But we must do more than this. We must recognise how unfair that relationship is to the working class, with so many influences weighing upon the worker, forcing him to accept a passive role, not acting but acted upon. Like the working men of Robert Tressell's *The Ragged Trousered Philanthropists*, Orwell's workers tend instinctively to believe that certain freedoms are 'not for the likes of us'. The educated middle class, by contrast, experience no such limitations; they expect to get what they want, within reasonable limits, and they know how to set about getting it. Orwell describes an associated characteristic of working-class life as 'this business of petty inconvenience and indignity, of being kept waiting about'. He suggests that this has to do with low expectations but it has also to do with poor verbal skills. Working people are frequently insufficiently articulate to play the kind of language game that might secure better service or quicker treatment. Dealing with these general issues Orwell establishes a background for the more systematic descriptive passages which follow — and he also wins our sympathy.

Housing is his first specific subject and although he has the statistics and factual detail to illustrate his arguments, it is the off-the-cuff generalisation emerging from the detail that captures our attention. Great numbers of the houses he describes are quite simply not fit to live in. Yet people live in them and consider themselves lucky, because there aren't enough of even these dreadful places. Orwell shows himself aware of the limitations of council redevelopment, complaining that the new corporation housing estates are soulless and life in them barren and regimented. While he disavows any sympathy with G. K. Chesterton's enthusiasm for slum life, where every man might be king of his own castle however mean, he does show a clear ambivalence, concluding that the corporation estates were marginally better than the slums — clean, decent houses being better than insanitary homes. He nevertheless advances a proposition which is very reminiscent of Chesterton: 'I sometimes think that the price of liberty is not so much eternal vigilance as eternal dirt.'[30]

Orwell's next theme is unemployment, and he begins by dispelling what he clearly considers to be a common middle-class misconception: that if statistics say that two million are unemployed they mean that two million people do not have enough to eat. Not so. This figure not only ignores those who have never registered but, more important, it ignores dependants. Quoting government sources, Orwell estimates that the total number of underfed people would be well over ten million.[31] He fills out this identification of the extent of poverty with a statistical analysis of what the unemployed spend their money on. Again, though, it is the generalisation which captures our attention: it is not poverty that destroys the unemployed so much as the loss of self-esteem. They no longer contribute to the community, no longer provide for their families: they are no longer men.[32] Orwell's intention is to engage not merely our understanding but our sympathy, and so he confronts the apparently anti-social decision of unemployed people to marry. This is proof only of good sense: losing you job does not mean that you cease to be human, he says, whatever the 'old ladies in Brighton' might think.

Orwell now moves on to a more general discussion about the nature of working-class life in the North, based upon his observations. He begins by identifying the North as a region defined by industrial squalor and ugliness – 'so frightful and so arresting that you are obliged, as it were, to come to terms with it'. Sheffield, for example, is described quite uncompromisingly as the ugliest town in the Old World. Orwell wants to confront his middle-class, predominantly Southern readership with the realisation that this industrial dereliction is qualitatively different from the down-at-heel inner-city areas of the South with which they may be familiar. Having set out his case Orwell poses two questions. Is is inevitable, this ugliness, and does it matter? His answer is that it matters chiefly because of the exploitative nature of what it represents. It is possible to build factories that are, if not actually aesthetically pleasing, at least neutral; but the underlying sense of the domination of a whole class of people which the factory system implies would still exist. It is with these people, the dominated, that he now concerns himself.

We have already briefly considered the common charge that Orwell romanticised the working class, and will turn to that issue in greater depth later on, but for the present it is worth making the point that Orwell made every attempt to demystify popular romantic images of

49

the workers before attempting to put in place his own myths and symbols. Here Orwell seeks to create an image of the Northern working class as possessing values and a way of living which is morally superior to that of many of his readers. But first he must cut the North down to size. He sets up in order to destroy it the common myth of Northern superiority in which 'you and I and everyone else in the south of England is written off as "fat and sluggish" '. Southerners, when they travel North, do so with an inferiority complex. Not so the Northerner coming South: 'the Yorkshireman, like the Scotchman, comes to London in the spirit of a barbarian out for loot'. Having dismissed all such distinctions as cant and anachronism, Orwell then proceeds to draw his own distinction, which is that of equality. In a memorable phrase he compares a Lancashire cotton town, where one could go for months without hearing a 'posh' accent to towns in the South 'where you could hardly throw a brick without hitting the niece of a bishop'. In one of his best-known passages Orwell seeks to describe, for his largely middle-class readership, the atmosphere of a working-class household (in which, importantly, the father is at work). Here one breathes 'a warm, decent, deeply human atmosphere which is not so easy to find elsewhere'. Home life for working people has a sane and pleasing symmetry.

Orwell was not a trained sociologist: what he gives us is a picture and not the tabulated and correlated results of a survey; yet it is hard to doubt that this image of symmetry and of people at their ease influenced his thought enormously. He believed that working-class life was not dominated by social or financial considerations, knew that it was not uprooted by the social and geographical mobility which puts middle-class family life so often at risk, and saw finally that it was integrated into a community life where the same values of togetherness or equality dominated. In short, Orwell believed that he had discovered, amongst the better-off working class, the secret of the good life. How to spread the message?

Orwell begins Part Two of *Wigan Pier*, overtly at least, by explaining what an important learning process his trip North had been. What he really has in mind is to take us on that journey with him. He exposes his own dislike and distrust of the working class in order that we recognise *ours*. He identifies himself with the 'shabby-genteel' middle class who, because of socially induced expenditure (keeping up appearances) are really no better off than the well-to-do working class. By taking refuge in some supposed cultural superiority this class keep the working class at arm's length, forbidding its children to play with the children of workers (as his own mother had done), sustaining a myth of the physical danger of visiting working-class areas. Above all, Orwell went on conspiratorially (in a section which caused the most unfavourable reaction), the basic difference between decent folk and the working class was that the latter were supposed to smell. There is no doubt that Orwell was unusually sensitive and fastidious about these matters, but there would be little point in making expiation in such a public and offensive way had he not believed that he was speaking for his class; this was vicarious expiation for everyone 'who has grown up pronouncing his aitches'.[33]

Well, he asks, is it true? The answer is ambiguous but may be summarised as 'not really'; not so as to matter, that is. He tells us: look, I have shared a bed with a tramp, drunk tea from the same tin, and it is really not important. He deals with the matter at considerable length for he sees it as fundamentally damaging that even those of the middle class who are socialists or communists should feel themselves crucially – chasmically as he so graphically puts is – divided from those whose interests they purport to champion.

At this point Orwell tries to create a rapport with his readers by offering a potted autobiography charting his own political development.[34] This autobiography does not match very closely the picture that has emerged here in previous chapters; probably he was seeking to establish his credentials with an audience many of whom were sympathetic to socialism. In the process he provided an ideological theme to his early career which was never as strongly marked as he suggests. In a sense, too, he may be rationalising, making a pattern out of past events from his new vantage point. Perhaps he had indeed come to see that his adult life constituted simply a long and hard march to Wigan Pier. At any rate the socialists and sympathisers amongst the readership were supposed to conclude that Orwell was one of them.

Are socialists serious about getting rid of class divisions? Of course not, says Orwell. The British standard of living is based upon the capitalistic exploitation of the native peoples of the empire, and socialists (like others) acquiesce in this every time they drink a cup of tea. In any case, class distinctions are notoriously difficult to eradicate. 'All my notions – notions of good or evil, of pleasant and unpleasant, of funny and serious, of ugly and beautiful – are essentially *middle-class* notions.' If a middle-class person wishes to abolish class distinctions then he or she must change his or her attitude to life or remain an active or potential exploiter. Yet few socialists seem even aware of the problem. They speak of levelling up, not levelling down, but this surely is simply another form of exploitation – obliging the workers to adopt middle-class standards.

Finally, and at some length, Orwell discusses the relationship be- tween the working-class and socialism as a political system. He begins with two assertions which clear the decks for action. First he states that socialism as a world system offers a way out of the exploiter/ exploited impasse; indeed socialism is 'such elementary common sense that I am sometimes amazed that it has not established itself already'.[35] Yet depite the fact that every empty belly is an argument for socialism, it seems to be becoming less and not more popular. Secondly Orwell claims for himself the role of devil's advocate, so that we may be confident that he is criticising socialism for its own good.

Why has the working class not turned towards socialism? One reason: its adherents. 'One sometimes gets the impression,' says Or- well in one of his most memorable sentences, 'that the mere words ''socialism'' and ''communism'' draw towards them with magnetic force every fruit-juice drinker, nudist, sandal wearer, sex maniac, Quaker, ''nature cure'' quack, pacifist and feminist in England.' These adherents, 'drawn towards the smell of ''progress'' like bluebottles to a dead cat', may dispose people, especially working people, against socialism but they are essentially harmless. Not so the socialist ideolo- gue, for whom Orwell expresses contempt. He is not motivated by fellow-feeling but probably a sense of order which sees poverty as something to be abolished from above, even by violence.[36] For these intellectuals socialism did not constitute a revolutionary movement of the masses but a set of reforms which the clever ones were going to impose upon the lower orders. For full measure, add to all this, says Orwell, the fact that socialist writers, like Shaw and William Morris, have been 'dull, empty windbags', and we begin to understand why ordinary people are turned away from socialism, seeing it not as man- kind's best hope for the future but as some kind of doom 'which must be staved off as long as possible'.

Against all this stands the ordinary working-class socialist for whom socialism means principally better wages and working conditions, but who has little grasp of the deeper ideological implications of socialism.

His vision of a socialist future is prosaic and limited, but Orwell considers him a truer socialist than the intellectuals 'because he does remember, what the other so often forgets, that socialism means justice and common decency'.[37] Orwell compares the working-class socialist to the working-class Roman Catholics; the ordinary Catholic families live out their faith without concerning themselves with dogma; it takes an intellectual to be a true zealot. Though they can hardly open their mouths without uttering a heresy, Orwell tells us, they have *the heart of the matter* in them. And so it is with the working-class socialist.

But when working-class socialists looks at socialism as an ideology, and at the ideologues, they recoil. To begin with, they see socialism as an urban creed, bound up with making machine-production more efficient. The socialist world is seen as an ordered and efficient world; a world in which nothing – or not much, at any rate – goes wrong. The goal of progress is to render humanity less than human – and the tragedy is that progress and socialism are inextricably linked in most people's minds (thanks in no small measure to the popularity of writers like H. G. Wells).

Not only is the idea of progress anathema to ordinary people, but also increased technical specialisation will lead, willy-nilly, to the rule of the expert, indeed to the 'beehive state'. Yes, of course, we all like the idea of an easier life in which unpleasant tasks are performed by machines, but in a deeper sense we want 'a civilisation in which "progress" is not definable as making the world safe for little fat men'. It is for all these reasons that many people turn away from socialism. If socialism, 'real' socialism, is the only effective answer to fascism, it is not the socialism of mechanisation and 'progress', not the socialism of thesis, antithesis and synthesis (the old pea and thimble trick), not the socialism of the planner, the intellectual or the sandal wearer and pacifist, but the socialism of ordinary people. Only they hold firmly to the 'underlying ideals of socialism: justice and liberty',[38] which alone can withstand fascism. 'Socialism,' he argues, 'at least in this island, does not smell any longer of revolution and the overthow of tyrants; it smells of crankishness, machine worship and the stupid cult of Russia.' Things must change or fascism may win.

It is hardly surprising that a call to arms which expressly excludes the bulk of the officer class would not find favour throughout the army, yet we cannot doubt that Orwell is deadly serious in his quest to win

over 'normal decent people' to the socialist cause. The socialist movement, he said, should not be 'a league of dialectical materialists but a
league of the oppressed against the oppressors'.[39]

How to accomplish this feat? Socialism had to capture and not frighten
away the exploited amongst the middle class, for potentially they have
far more in common with the working class than with the 'oppressors'.
Indeed in a more passioned tone Orwell is reiterating a plea made by
Lloyd George to socialists during the pre-First World War elections
when he told his audiences that an overtly class-based socialist party
would frighten the middle classes into reaction and Toryism. Orwell
believed that the millions of lower-middle-class people, though they too
were robbed and bullied by the same system could, if faced with a choice,
side with the oppressors rather than with their natural allies. So the
socialist movement has to demonstrate exactly where the cleavage
between the exploiters and the exploited comes. This means stripping
socialism back to its essentials, getting rid of those socialists (almost
invariably bourgeois themselves) who engage in bourgeois baiting. If it
fails to do so, and here he echoes Lloyd George almost precisely, many of
the middle class would turn to the Right: 'if you frighten them into
combining *against* you, you may find that you have raised up a devil'.[40] As
for the middle class, the message was simple: let us join the working
class, where we actually belong, 'for, after all, we have nothing to lose
but our aitches'.

Thus in this extraordinary book Orwell established the main structure of his political thought. He has a view of socialism as a living value
system, a system which forms the basis of working-class life in the North
of England. It is a system which is rooted in equality and which empha-
sises what might be called the basic Judaeo-Christian civic virtues of
decency and justice. This system has been warped and manipulated
almost beyond recognition by socialist intellectuals whose understanding of social relationships is economic and ideological and not human,
and who do not understand or necessarily even like the working class.
Orwell was to expand on this view continually during the next fifteen
years but basically not to change it. In fact his Spanish experiences, as
well as providing him with many new political insights, were to crystal-
lise many of the views expressed here, as we shall now see.

When Orwell arrived in Spain the anarchists were still in control of
Catalonia and he joined the militia in December 1936 in Barcelona. He
received a startling impression of the town. Practically every building

was draped with red or red and black flags, every wall hosting a hammer and sickle or the initials of one of the revolutionary parties. All the churches – for the Church was seen to be the ally of the fascists – were gutted, all the cafés and shops collectivised. Tipping was forbidden, there were no private motor cars and all the trams and taxis were painted red and black. In the Ramblas, the main thoroughfare, loudspeakers gave out revolutionary songs. Apart from a few foreigners, says Orwell, there were no well-dressed people at all, practically everybody wore blue overalls.

> Nobody said *'Senor'* or *'Don'* or even *'Usted'*; everyone called everyone else 'Comrade' and 'thou', and said *'Salud!'* instead of *'Buenos Dias'* [sic]. . . It was the first time that I had ever been in a town where the working class was in the saddle . . . There was much in it that I did not understand, in some ways I did not even like it, but I recognized it immediately as a state of affairs worth fighting for . . . because human beings were trying to behave like human beings and not as cogs in the capitalist machine.[41]

Orwell's great sympathy for the Spanish working class is conveniently forgotten by those who dismiss his socialism as quintessentially English. Indeed the defining characteristic which he ascribed to the Spanish workers is essential decency and 'a real largeness of spirit which I have met with again and again in the most unpromising circumstances.' For Orwell the Spanish civil war was originally a war between democratic socialism (one might almost say Orwellian socialism) and fascism; that it manifestly became something other than this saddened him greatly. In many respects it reinforced his conclusion about the role of intellectuals and ideologues and underlined his argument that only the working class could stand against fascism. He came to believe that the centralised, efficient state which the communists wished to create was only marginally better than fascism. That such a discovery should make him bitter and desperate to make it widely known is not difficult to understand. After all, as late as December 1936 he had dismissed 'the vulgar lie, now so popular, that "communism and fascism are the same thing" '.[42]

Orwell concluded *Homage to Catalonia*, after recounting his sad story of disillusionment and betrayal, by harking back to much the same claims with which he had concluded *Wigan Pier*: the just demands of the working class – everywhere. He supports the workers' materialism, for it consitutes only a demand for the basic needs of a decent life. He rejected the 'squalid farce of left-wing politics', along with Russian communism, British equivocation ('its democratic phrases and its coolie empire') in support of the struggle of the poor for justice against the exploiters and their lackeys. 'I myself believe, perhaps on insufficient grounds, that the common man will win his fight sooner or later, but I want it to be sooner and not later . . . .'[43]

4 The world set free

Bearing in mind that the young Etonian Blair was said to see himself as a new Shaw, it is interesting to compare the mature Orwell's attitude towards political action with that of his early model. Shaw was a man of ideas for whom men of action held an intrinsic appeal. He himself was not a man of action, not a man who thrilled to the rumble of the tumbrils' wheels. Orwell, in stark contrast, was a man whose ideas crystallised on the barricades, a man for whom taking sides was all. When the so-called phoney war came to an end and France was crumbling under the weight of the blitzkrieg, Orwell declared himself a patriot. He had dreamt some year earlier, he said, of war coming and had wakened knowing that the British government, even under Chamberlain, was assured of his loyalty, to the extent of fighting if possible.[1] On the face of it this was a sudden and almost complete volte-face for a man who had not long before declared that Western capitalism was only a subtler form of fascism. If the dream story is to be believed however, the suddenness at least may be more apparent than real. As we have seen, Orwell's conviction that war had become inevitable was reinforced by the Nazi-Soviet pact. The luxury of supporting all the exploited against all the exploiters was no longer an option. It had to be admitted that not all exploitation was the same and after all, half a loaf was not the same as no bread. Orwell declared that although his patriotism might be largely the result of the brainwashing of a bourgeois education system, he could also persuade himself that he might look forward with some degree of confidence to revolutionary changes in Britain, with the gutters of London running with blood and the red militias billeted at the Ritz. More of this later. In the meantime, however, the only alternative to fighting the Nazis was surrender.

Orwell would gladly have relinquished the pen for the sword, indeed would have seized with both hands *any* opportunity to participate in *any* effective way in the war effort. 'Everything is disintegrating,' he wrote, 'it makes me writhe to be writing book reviews at such a time.'² His medical history, however, ruled out action.

If Orwell could not help the war effort directly, Eileen could. She took a job in the censorship department in Whitehall and appeared at Wallington only at weekends. This proved a considerable help to family finances but the long hours and the travelling exhausted her. For his part Orwell, still looking unavailingly for something positive to do, spent his time taking care of the animals and working on his essays. At the end of the year he joined Eileen in London and, amidst the alarms and excursions, managed to complete a collection of what were to become some of his most celebrated major essays, *Inside the Whale*. It was published in March 1940 to wide acclaim. The period immediately after was a somewhat fallow one by Orwell's standards. He told friends that he had written enough in recent years and needed a break but told others, inconsistently, that he was so busy reviewing that he simply could not find time to start on anything substantial. An autobiographical note which he prepared for an American directory concluded with the observation that he was preparing a long novel in three parts.³ Whatever was visualised, and whether his last two novels comprised parts of it, must remain conjectural. No large-scale work in three parts was ever produced or indeed even sketched out. On the more private level, the Orwells decided to shut up Wallington and move to London, with Orwell himself becoming theatre critic for *Time and Tide* and reviewing regularly both for this journal and for *Tribune*.

These were among the darkest days of the war. The British Expeditionary Force had escaped from Dunkirk in total disarray and Orwell wrote in his newly-kept diary of its arrival in London from the Channel ports in dribs and drabs. For the Orwells this national tragedy was personalised by the death of Laurence O'Shaughnessy, killed on the Dunkirk beaches while looking after the wounded. It was a bitter blow for the distraught Eileen; she had come to rely totally on her brother, who had provided a bedrock of emotional and practical support during Orwell's illnesses. Eileen fell into a depression from which she recovered only with the adoption of their son almost three years later. For health reasons and also because he cared more for his writing than he did for individuals (himself included), Eileen could hardly rely on her husband in the same measure. It is strange that no mention of Laurence O'Shaughnessy's death appears in Orwell's diary. Both Crick and Shelden wonder whether this might not imply some lack of feeling on Orwell's part but since the diary was intended for publication perhaps the author believed that his role as witness might be compromised by a retreat into personal grief. Ironically, if Laurence had lived he could have done nothing to save his sister but his expertise might have proved invaluable to Orwell himself.

Orwell had by no means given up his attempt to join up, but the nearest he came to success was the Local Defence Volunteers (which became the Home Guard) in June 1940. At the back of his mind was at least half an expectation that these groups would form the front line in the revolutionary struggle. (Perhaps he had forgotten an incident from Koestler's *The Gladiators*, which he had reviewed earlier, when one of the towns under siege from Spartacus' slave army had defended itself by arming its own slaves against their brothers.) At the same time he tried to secure some bureaucratic role in the war machine but to no avail. He felt that his service with the republican side in the Spanish Civil War probably made him a security risk.[4]

At this time Orwell began to write regularly for the monthly *Horizon*, and not long after for the American left-wing journal, *Partisan Review*. Cyril Connolly affectionately pointed out that Orwell was very much at home during these disastrous years.[5] He thrived on the physical danger of the bombs and British defeats could only mean the eventual overthrow of Churchill and the advent of a revolutionary socialist government. Connolly may have been right – it is in keeping with Orwell's character – yet his writing suggests the more traditional view of these days as a drab, dispiriting and unequal struggle against fearful conditions, including a shortage of food.

To what extent was Orwell buoyed up by a faith in the coming revolution? It is clear that his involvement with the Home Guard soon became much more than a *pis aller*, and he did not think of its activities in 'Dad's Army' terms in the slightest. All the same, the onlooker might see certain similarities. Because no precise task in the event of the impending invasion was originally allotted to it, the Home Guard could hardly engage in any specific training. Weapon drill would have been possibile but in the early days it had no weapons. Moreover for the most part those who trained the Guard were veterans from the Flanders trenches. Orwell was not prepared to accept this state of affairs. He wrote a letter in *Time and Tide*[6] urging the arming of the Home Guard specifically with hand-grenades but also with shotguns and whatever else could be requisitioned. He continued with a list of practical suggestions, a number of which were soon to be introduced by the government (though not as a result of his influence). Elsewhere and for a different audience, he wrote that the regular army was not the only model for the Home Guard; a democratic guerrilla force offered an alternative much more attractive to socialists. Writing in *Tribune*[7] Orwell pointed out that if a few thousand socialists were to join the Home Guard and show to their comrades in arms that it was possible to be both a patriot and a socialist, the nature of this force could be transformed. The influence of such men, thought Orwell, amongst an increasingly armed group of ordinary British men, could be enormous. Orwell wrote in similar terms on a number of occasions, including a centre-page spread in the London *Evening Standard*. 'The totalitarian states,' he wrote, 'can do great things, but there is one thing they cannot do: they cannot give the factory-worker a rifle and tell him to take it home and keep it in the bedroom. That rifle . . . is the symbol of democracy.'[8] There is an obvious inconsistency in Orwell's thought here, which he is either unaware of or is incapable of resolving. The ruling class can arm the workers only and precisely because they know that a socialist revolution is not feasible and Orwell must have been aware of this fact himself. If the workers ever were to use their rifles against the ruling class then surely they would have abused what he himself recognised as the symbol of democracy. Orwell wished to associate socialism with patriotism and yet must have realised that the overwhelming majority of his compatriots would see socialist revolution as inimical to patriotism. Indeed in his advice to socialists to join, he specifically warns that the spreading of subversive opinions in the Home Guard would be 'both treacherous and ineffective'. Totalitarian leaders, it seemed, were not the only people unable to tolerate rifles in citizens' bedrooms. Eileen too put her foot down: 'I can put up with bombs on the mantelpiece but I will not have a machine gun under the bed.'[9]

Among a number of like-minded intellectuals in London at the time was Tosco Fyvel, with whom Orwell edited a series of pamphlets called 'Searchlight Books'. The task of the series was to popularise discussion about war aims (which meant spreading the message of democratic socialism), and we can assume that these pamphlets had a ready if somewhat specialist market. Moreover, it was as part of this series that Orwell published one of his most important works, and one which set out his political philosophy as clearly as anything else, *The Lion and the Unicorn*, to which we shall be returning later.

Orwell served in the Home Guard for three years as a sergeant and had under his guard, among others, Fredric Warburg who was to write about life as a corporal to Orwell's sergeant in an autobiography.[10] For all that Orwell's men may have missed on the parade ground, they more than made up for in training in street fighting. Naturally enough, as the fear of invasion withered and with it hopes for a democratic vanguard emerging from the Home Guard, so did Orwell's enthusiasm, and he resigned on medical grounds in late 1943. Not, of course, without urging a post-war role for a more democratically organised Home Guard as a replacement for the Territorial Army.[11]

During 1942 Orwell's sister Avril and his mother (now nearly sixty-seven) moved up to London. They were able to provide occasional comfort for Eileen, though they had principally come to work to help the war effort. In March 1943, however, Ida Blair, who had been suffering poor health, was taken into hospital. She died one week later. Among the causes of death were listed acute bronchitis and emphysema. It seems to have been his mother's death which prompted Orwell to take the plunge and consider adopting a child.

Service with the Home Guard did not constitute Orwell's only contribution to the war effort. In the autumn of 1941 he was offered a contract with the BBC as temporary talks producer in the empire department: he became part of the propaganda machine. He was only one of a number of intellectuals called to the colours, including Louis MacNeice and William Empson. After a year as producer, in which he became responsible for a weekly news commentary which went out to India, it was suggested that Orwell should actually deliver the talks himself; after all, he was already delivering a weekly news summary to Singapore. His immediate superior thought that having 'Orwell' speaking directly to India would, in itself, be a considerable propaganda gain and he raised the matter first with the writer himself. Orwell agreed, but only on the condition that he be allowed 'reasonable freedom of speech' (his phrase) and, more specifically, allowed to adopt an 'anti-fascist rather than imperialist' standpoint and not to adopt any pro-government line with which he was not himself in sympathy. There was no opposition to this and Orwell set about organising an impressive array of talent to inform Indian intellectuals. Orwell's throat wound had left him an ineffectual speaker; his broadcasts went out at an inauspicious time of day and young Indian intellectuals, at whom they were mostly aimed, tended not to possess radios.

Although he can scarcely have deluded himself on these matters, there were clearly other aspects of his work which Orwell found appealing, including the company of Empson in the China section, and Muggeridge. Life at the BBC had its compensations and he stood it for two years, leaving in the autumn of 1943 because, as he said in his letter of resignation, he felt he was wasting his own time and taxpayers' money 'on doing work that produces no result'.[12] He believed that his journalism, by contrast, did 'produce some measurable effect'.

Before he left the BBC there was some talk of his going to North Africa as a war correspondent for the *Observer*, though this was to prove impossible since at the time war correspondents were attached to the army and had to be medically fit. By the time this plan had to be given up, however, another opportunity had presented itself: he was offered the literary editorship of *Tribune*.

It would be hard to think of a more suitable job for Orwell, given that participating in the war directly was out of the question. Although the salary was less than he had earned with the BBC, he was obliged actually to go in to work on only three days each week, leaving him more time for his writing.

The editorial directors of the paper at that time were the Labour MPs George Strauss and Aneurin Bevan, both independent-minded – indeed somewhat rebellious – and both prepared to leave the running of the paper to the editor. Crick speaks of the *Tribune* as possessing a distinctive style of argument rather than a definitive editorial policy or 'line'. Others might imagine that this added up to pretty much the same thing, but the important point is that it provided not so much a controlled environment as a natural habitat for Orwell, and he flourished as a consequence. Also about this time he began to write regularly for the *Observer*, having struck up a friendship with David Astor the editor and son of the owner, who admired Orwell's work greatly. He continued his reviewing, too, and indeed on a grander scale than ever. Although it would appear that he must have dissipated his energies on these exercises, it is clear that he used his journalism and reviewing to explore aspects of the grand themes which were to dominate his last two books.

From Orwell's own point of view his 'As I Please' column for *Tribune* was a wonderful opportunity to explore facets of his personality, especially his love of the countryside and his sentimental, nostalgic attachment to the certainties of pre-1914 English family and community life, which were to be used as yardsticks to measure the horrors of life on Animal Farm and in Oceania. Crick identified 232 separate subjects of Orwell's column during his days as editor, but most were directly or indirectly political in nature. He was criticised by readers in about equal measure for frivolous self-indulgence and anti-Soviet attitudes. Fortunately for Orwell he enjoyed the support of Bevan, but it is instructive to hear from Crick that neither Strauss nor Michael Foot (who replaced Bevan as editor in 1945) could remember whether Orwell's column was included in the literary or political section of the paper. He concludes: 'Orwell . . . *did* do very much as he pleased, and his failure to pay attention to the conventional distinction between politics and literature has perpetually irritated some and pleased others.'[13]

It is typical of Orwell that he almost always responded to serious letters, whether from the famous or the unknown, and often at considerable length. He was thus able to develop his main ideas and analyse and reassess them as a consequence of comments and criticisms. In his position as literary editor he was able to meet many of the leading left-wing intellectual figures of the day on a social basis; more opportunity to have his ideas discussed. No wonder that his days at the *Tribune* were among Orwell's happiest and most fruitful. At the same time he knew that this period would be temporary, indeed relatively short; he was talking of moving to the country after the war, indeed referred specifically to the Hebrides, its distance from London clearly being a major attraction.

Was Orwell a good literary editor? Tosco Fyvel, who replaced him, inherited a deskful of unacknowledged manuscripts and commissioned but unused articles. Others have suggested that he was far too soft in handling unsolicited material, accepting what a more realistic editor would have politely declined. Orwell was unrepentantly aware of his own limitations. Perhaps those who have spent a long time as a freelance journalist ought never to become an editor, he thought. 'It is too like taking a convict out of his cell and making him governor of the prison.'[14]

Almost at the same time as he started his editorial career Orwell began work on *Animal Farm*. He was clear from the beginning that it was to be a short book and that it might prove politically controversial; he was equally clear, it seems, that it would be followed by a book along similar lines to Zamyatin's *We*.[15] In other words he was planning his work more systematically than had been his practice previously, and the continuity between his last two books – the revolution and the post-revolution – was not accidental. Not only was Orwell more systematic but he was also involving Eileen much more, reading pages to her, asking and taking her advice. And what is more, when the book was finally finished Orwell was more than satisfied with the result. '*Animal Farm*', he was later to write, 'was the first book in which I tried, with the full consciousness of what I was doing, to fuse political purpose and artistic purpose into one whole.'[16] He knew that he had succeeded. When he had finished the book in March of 1944 Orwell not only had no doubts as to its merit, he also had no doubts as to its reception on the left. In fact he wrote to Gollancz explaining that though he was willing to send him the typescript it would prove 'completely unacceptable politically from your point of view'. Gollancz replied that he would like to see the typescript and could not understand Orwell's misgivings. The typescript was duly sent, with a request for a speedy reaction. It came. In a matter of days Gollancz wrote: 'You were right and I was wrong. I am so sorry. I have returned the manuscript . . . .'[17] Jonathan Cape, to whom Orwell's agent subsequently sent the typescript, also rejected it. They had taken the precaution of giving it to a senior official in the Ministry of Information to look at, and his advice had been that to publish the book could only do great damage to the relationship with Britain's war-time ally, the Soviet Union. Orwell then sent a copy personally to T. S. Eliot at Faber and here, too, it was rejected, though Eliot thought it among the best work of its kind since *Gulliver's Travels*. He also reflected that although it was clear whom Orwell was attacking in the book, it was not so clear from which side. In practical terms this was a disadvantage since, the time being inauspicious for an attack on the Soviet Union, it was necessary to have a constituency – and Orwell had none. Eliot's own surmise was that Orwell's position was Trotskyist, though not convincingly so. Although Warburg had expressed an interest in publishing the book in some form or other (at this stage of the war paper was a problem) Orwell chose not to pursue the possibility.

Orwell had expected to encounter these problems but he began to grow frustrated, imagining that either Gollancz or the Ministry of Information (or indeed both) were quietly warning London publishers off. However, he could not have anticipated the reasoning behind the rejection from the Dial Press in the United States, who turned the book down because 'it was impossible to sell animal stories in the USA'.[18] Although originally he had hoped to have the book brought out by a prestigious publisher, he seemed to have settled on having it published by a one-man-band when Warburg finally decided to take the book on. Although publication by a quality press was now assured, there were to be production difficulties and *Animal Farm* did not finally appear until August 1945, by which time the war had come to an end: a fact which Orwell refused to believe was coincidental.

In June of 1943 Eileen gave up her job with the Ministry of Food and the Orwells adopted a son, Richard Horatio. Their life took on a new dimension and, as can be imagined, Orwell took delight in the chores of fatherhood. But his knack of inviting disaster did not desert him even on the domestic front, for on June 28th their flat was damaged by a doodlebug (flying bomb), which had struck nearby, and although none of them was hurt they had to move out. After borrowing a friend's flat they rented a pleasant place of their own but already began enquiries about somewhere in the country, where their son could grow up. David Astor owned property on the Isle of Jura and was able to put Orwell in contact with the owner of a remote farmhouse on the island which she was prepared to let cheaply. He went up to see the house and Eileen began to correspond with the owner about what they would need. For Orwell the realisation of an ambition cherished for some time was coming much closer.[19]

He was by no means idle following the acceptance of *Animal Farm*; he had begun to put together a collection of essays which he finished in January 1945. These were to be published as *Critical Essays* and included previous work then out of print, such as the essays on Dickens and boys' weeklies, a selection of his pieces from *Horizon*, together with new essays. In a number of these he was working out themes which were going to become central to *Nineteen Eighty-four*: power as an end and not a means, the inadequacy of hedonism as a motor for political action, and the link between violence and totalitarianism.

Despite his productivity, despite his continually failing health (and that of his wife), despite his efforts to find a Hebridean home, and despite his new domestic commitments, Orwell seized with relish the opportunity offered by David Astor (one or other of them seems to have circumvented the health obstacles which had precluded Orwell's earlier involvement) to act as a war correspondent for the *Observer* and cover the liberation of France and the invasion of Germany. By the middle of March he was off to Paris.

At his hotel in Paris Orwell met, among others, Ernest Hemingway, P. G. Wodehouse and, at some leisure, the philosopher A. J. Ayer. He moved on after a few weeks to Germany but became ill in Cologne, seriously enough to draw up and send to Eileen a document of instructions for his 'literary executor'. Eileen was never to receive it; she herself had died, at the age of only thirty-nine, two days before it was sent. Orwell received the news by wire from the *Observer* and immediately discharged himself from hospital. With incredible speed and in very bad shape he returned to the United Kingdom, travelling almost immediately up to the North East, where Eileen had gone with Richard after his departure for France.

Death was no stranger to Orwell. He was, it must be said, a man dedicated above all things to his work, and his marriage, moreover, had not given him everything he had been looking for. But the loss of this charming, supportive and in many ways brilliant woman, with whom he had been through so much, must have pole-axed him. Orwell knew Eileen's operation was pending,[20] knew too that it was almost certainly of a more serious nature than he seemed prepared to admit later. In a letter to a friend, Eileen had written that she had been pleased to have travelled north because the operation to remove 'the tumours', as part of a hysterectomy, would be undertaken without the period of 'fattening up' which, she claimed, London doctors insisted upon before operating. She knew that there were other reasons far more sinister than regional fashion for the urgency. Crick and Shelden show from the relevant correspondence that there had been some disagreement between Orwell and his wife about the need for the operation and perhaps the cost of it. Moreover both of them were sincerely concerned that if Eileen were to admit to a long-term illness then Richard's adoption, which was about to be formalised, might not go through. There seems no reason to doubt that the decision to postpone the operation was anything other than a tragic miscalculation on Orwell's and Eileen's parts, in which case his despair must have been complete. He must have taken some very small consolation, however, from the fact that Eileen's death was entirely unexpected and not a direct consequence of her illness (cardiac failure while under anaesthetic, read the death certificate) or any part that he may have had in her delaying seeking treatment.

After the funeral, and having made temporary arrangements for Richard, Orwell went back to Europe, more to come to terms with things than for any professional reason. Indeed it is true to say that, thoroughly competent though his reporting was, his few months in Europe produced no writing of any great note. He was back in the United Kingdom in June, in time for the election campaign, about which he chose to write little. He threw himself into journalistic work, writing regularly now for the *Observer, Manchester Evening News* and *Tribune*, to a degree that gave his friends cause for concern. In the year after Eileen's death he wrote more than 130 articles and reviews.[21] His loneliness was acute and within the same year he proposed to at least four women, each of whom rejected him. Amongst them was Sonia Brownwell, of whom he had begun to see quite a lot. Sonia was a dynamic young woman, a friend of artists and writers, who worked as Cyril Connolly's editorial assistant on *Horizon*, and who was much sought after. According to Crick, Sonia found Orwell 'the only intellectual she knew who could mend a fuse';[22] she was impressed by his sincerity and must have been aware of his growing fame. Sonia, too, had been born in India, though she was very young when she came to Britain after the death of her father. It is not difficult to imagine what Orwell saw in her. She was a very tough-minded young woman; Shelden tells of a boating accident which befell Sonia while at finishing school in Switzerland. She and three companions had capsized a boat in the middle of a lake. Her three companions drowned. Sonia later revealed to her family, though not to the Swiss police, that she tried to save one young man but he had struggled and she had held his head under the water to stop him; he never came up.[23] It is almost certain that Sonia was the model for Julia in *Nineteen Eighty-four*; Julia, who declared herself to be 'corrupt to the bones' and who, when Winston described the temptation to push his wife off a cliff, replied: 'Why didn't you give her a good shove? I would have.' 'Yes, dear,' Winston retorted, 'you would have.' Orwell and Sonia had a brief affair, which she found unsatisfying.

He was also very impressed by Celia Kirwan, Arthur Koestler's sister-in-law, and proposed to her, too, in a typically matter-of-fact manner, pointing out all the potential disadvantages of the arrangement. Although she turned him down (much to Koestler's disappointment) they remained friends until his death. One of the other young women to whom Orwell proposed later received letters from him expanding on his very precipitate proposal in terms which indicate his state of mind at the time:

> I do so want someone who will share what is left of my life, and my work
> . . . If I can live another ten years I think I have another three worthwhile
> books left in me, besides a lot of odds and ends, but I want peace and quiet
> and somebody to be fond of me.[24]

This is straightforward and honest but hardly loving.

On August 17th 1945 *Animal Farm* was published. The first impression of only 4,500 copies very quickly sold out and it was not until November that a second impression, this time of 10,000 copies, came out. 25,000 copies were sold within five years. In America 590,000 were sold in four years. In the last 47 years it has never stopped printing. Almost overnight Orwell became a household name. When Queen Elizabeth sent the royal messenger to Secker and Warburg for a copy of the book, they were sold out. He had to go, 'with horse, carriage, top hat and all, to the anarchist Freedom Bookshop in Red Lion Square [once home of the Marxist poet William Morris], where George Woodcock gave him a copy.'[25]

It is tempting to believe that Orwell must at this point have thought that all of his struggles, and indeed Eileen's, had proved worthwhile, but unless he is seen as a man bent upon fame, the temptation should be resisted. Instead we should consider what it was that Orwell was seeking to achieve in this period, and then perhaps consider the extent to which he had succeeded. To do this it will be necessary to look at Orwell's major works during the period in detail, beginning with *Homage to Catalonia*.

Had he been asked, when setting out for Spain, what he most hoped for from the next decade, Orwell would have opted not for personal fame but for a successful socialist revolution, and by this criterion the period was hardly a success. *Homage to Catalonia*, as we have seen, bore the seeds of both his hope and his disillusion. The book, which takes the form of a documentary account of Orwell's experiences during the Spanish civil war, opens with a symbolic meeting between the author himself and an Italian militiaman. He made an immediately favourable impression upon Orwell. They shook hands and it 'was as though his spirit and mine had momentarily succeeded in bridging the gulf of language and tradition'. Yet he instinctively realised that to retain his first impression he must not see the Italian again; and neither did he.

Here in the first page of the book is a symbol of the whole Spanish experience; indeed one might be tempted to say, the experienece of revolutionary socialism. Orwell recognised in the stranger's face a preparedness to murder or to throw away his own life for a friend, and hoped that the Italian will recognise something similar in his own face. They were bound together by a mutual commitment to a comradeship based upon a respect for feedom and equality. Yet at the same time Orwell understood that if they were really to get to know each other the strength of their relationship would be inevitably weakened, the fragility of their mutual regard exposed. These bonds, forged *in extremis*, may not be broken by death but they may be eaten away by familiarity. Put another way, they may survive hardship, even failure in the revolutionary enterprise, but they are unlikely to survive success. Another facet of the man's character which Orwell perceived was his ignorance and with it 'the pathetic reverence that illiterate people have for their supposed superiors'. False consciousness stalks, ready to steal the inheritance of the revolution.

The description of Barcelona itself provides a similar picture of exhilarating colour and a sense of purpose, with the loudspeakers blasting out the latest revolutionary songs, all the comrades in blue overalls or militia uniform, and no obviously well-to-do people to be seen.[26] Orwell was deeply touched by this town in which the working class was in the saddle. But of course he recognised its fragility. When he tells of illiterate militiamen buying ballad sheets about proletarian brotherhood, painstakingly spelling out and learning the words and then singing them, it would come as no surprise if the words to one turned out to be equivalent to: 'four legs good, two legs bad'. In the streets of the town were posters telling prostitutes not to be prostitutes now that socialism had arrived, again reminding us of the best intentions of the cats and rats on Animal Farm. To anyone from the 'hard-boiled sneering civilisation of the English-speaking races' all this was 'rather pathetic'. It seems that Orwell himself was not entirely convinced.

In *Homage to Catalonia* Orwell provides us with a full and clear account of the conflicting tensions between the principles which a revolution seeks to establish and the methods necessary actually to win the revolutionary struggle. It is not the longer-term concern, so incisively analysed in the debate between Ivanov and Rubashov in Koestler's *Darkness at Noon*,[27] but rather the concern of revolutionary strategy. Orwell's early experiences with POUM, a largely Trotskyist organisation, suggested a strong sense of purpose but a damaging lack of discipline. Yet familiarity allowed a more tolerant view. He came to see the militia as a 'temporary working model of the classless society'. It took far longer to instil revolutionary discipline because it was based upon political consciousness, upon an understanding of the reasoning behind orders and not simply upon doing as one was told: theirs to reason why.

Later Orwell was to meet men who had not acquired political consciousness. His response to encountering a detachment of Andalusians is telling: 'Few if any of them could read, and they seemed not to know the one thing that everybody knows in Spain – which party they belonged to.'[28] So much for political consciousness. Moreover, although by Second-World-War standards the Spanish civil war was primitive, it was always going to be won by efficiency, technical expertise and superior equipment, all advantages held by Franco's falangists. When battles had depended, among other things, upon the courage and tenacity of individual fighting men, then the principles which incited that courage and tenacity were of great importance, but battles won by technical superiority owe little to the personality of the military technician. This fundamental point was seized on by Wells, who had argued with typical bluster that the politics of equality had no future after battles had ceased to be won by ordinary men (for example the bowmen of Crecy). Orwell himself made a similar point, arguing that tanks, battleships and bombers were inherently tyrannical whereas hand-grenades and so on were democratic: they gave 'claws to the weak'.[29]

The argument concerning means and ends can be taken at a different level. It has frequently been observed that the distinction between means and ends is not a sustainable one.[30] If it is argued that the end for the republicans in Spain was the establishment of an egalitarian democracy then the civil war can be seen as a means. Yet the moment winning the war becomes a prime objective it in fact becomes the identifiable end, and under discussion then are the best means to achieve that end. For the revolutionary militias the war was just part of the revolutionary struggle against fascism in all its aspects on behalf of worker control of the state. So the war had to be fought and won on those terms. For the communists the more limited objective was simply to win the war and as Orwell points out, this led them to conclude:

'Whoever tries to turn the civil war into a social revolution is playing into the hands of the fascists and is in effect, if not in intention, a traitor.'[31] Orwell could see both points of view, though he freely acknowledged that, given the circumstances, the communists appeared to be the only people capable of winning the war on the republican side. 'The revolutionary purism of the POUM, though I saw its logic, seemed to me rather futile. After all, the one thing that mattered was to win the war.' Elsewhere he went even further and declared that he had given a more sympathetic account of POUM than he actually felt appropriate. He had always told them they were wrong, he said, and had refused to join the party. But he had to give them a sympathetic case because they 'had no hearing in the capitalist press and nothing but libels in the left-wing press'.[32]

Even so, he considered the efforts of the communists to discredit and even liquidate their revolutionary comrades-in-arms to be despicable, and not only because his own life was at stake. 'On paper the communist case was a good one,' he acknowledged, but 'the only trouble was that their actual behaviour made it difficult to believe that they were advancing it in good faith.' Perhaps the war was simply not worth winning on such conditions; perhaps it was, in the end, better to stay true to the original end, for the *idea* might survive.

A third tension thrown up by the revolutionary agenda was that between the nobility of the revolutionary cause and the sordid reality of the war. Chesterton had chided socialists for their self-confidence: they always *assumed* that they would win the class struggle,[33] but perhaps their opponents had not studied Marx. It had been long recognised by Marxists like William Morris, often regarded as a sentimentalist, that the socialist revolution might be bloody but it would be quick, decisive and victorious. That is how he depicted it in *News from Nowhere*.[34] Although it has become commonplace to confront the nationalists and militarists with the dire consequences of their ambitions – Remarque's *All Quiet on the Western Front* offering an obvious example – it has been far less common to confront the socialist revolutionary's equally romantic and equally dangerous ideas of the glories of the revolutionary struggle with harsh realities. Orwell's picture of the socialist revolution contains great heroism but it contains lies, treachery, confusion, boredom, brutality and defeat.

Perhaps Orwell expected all this; it is hard to imagine that he went to Spain with many illusions. What he clearly did not expect was the selective media coverage of events. Selective in the sense that the media not only chose what to report and what not to report but in the sense that what was reported bore a selective relation to the truth. In Spain he saw newspaper reports which were unrelated to the facts, 'not even the relationship which is implied in any ordinary lie . . . and I saw newspapers in London retailing these lies and eager intellectuals building emotional superstructures over events that had never happened'.[35] He found this development profoundly sinister because it portended the disappearance from the world of the 'very concept of objective truth'.

Finally, did Orwell return to Britain with any optimism left? An often-quoted comment he made to Cyril Connolly on his return seems to suggest that he did: he had seen wonderful things in Spain and returned 'believing' in socialism, which he had never done before.[36] This quotation is often used (incorrectly) to show that Orwell had not before considered himself a socialist. It is more likely that he was using the word 'believe' in a religious sense; that is the full acceptance, emotional and spiritual as well as intellectual, of a given truth. Orwell had seen wonderful things! He had joined the militia to fight for 'common decency' and, at the end of everything, his desire to see socialism established had been made 'much more actual than it had been before'. Spain confirmed Orwell's belief that only the working class and not the intellectuals or the ideologues were the true enemies of fascism, and, as we have seen, the Second World War allowed him to hope that the British working class would, in taking on Hitler, destroy its own latently fascist ruling class and establish an egalitarian socialist society.

After *Homage* came some of Orwell's most celebrated essays. That on Dickens is by far the longest and is both a literary and political commentary. The gist of the political commentary is to suggest that, for all its appeal, Dickens' work was limited by its lack of social and economic analysis, and yet paradoxially that lack was also one of its strengths. 'The vagueness of his discontent is the mark of its permanence,' he argued. Many have said of Orwell much the same as he himself said of Dickens: '[Dickens'] is the face of a man who is always fighting against something, but who fights in the open and is not frightened, the face of a man who is *generously angry*'. We shall be returning to this essay.

A second major essay, 'Inside the Whale', which examines the proper role of the writer in an overtly political age like the 1930s, again gives no hint of a changing political perspective on Orwell's part.

Without a doubt, however, the major example of the development of his political thinking of this period was the substantial essay, *The Lion and the Unicorn: Socialism and the English Genius*. He seeks to address the British people, whom he persists, after explanation but no apology, in referring to as 'the English', by suggesting what it is that sets them apart. We discover that the defining characteristic of British culture is its gentleness – bus conductors are good-tempered and policemen carry no revolvers. He elaborates on this theme, discerning a hatred of militarism. The battles which the British sing about, write about and remember are mostly defeats: Mons, Ypres, Gallipoli – and Dunkirk. 'The most stirring battle-poem in English is about a brigade of cavalry which charged in the wrong direction.' What Orwell was trying to do was to establish a bond with his readers so that he could conduct them towards ways of thinking they would not otherwise have ventured into. His conclusion is that for all its internal divisions, Britain is still 'a family. It has its private language and its common memories, and at the approach of an enemy it closes ranks. A family with the wrong members in control . . . .'

Orwell's task was to establish that there was no fundamental dichotomy between this, the 'English genius', and socialist revolution; in fact to establish precisely the opposite. He attempts this by linking the aims of socialist revolution to the British sense of decency, but also to victory in the war against Hitler. His is no longer the 'old-fashioned' idea of the proletarian revolution; his is no longer the idea of 'red flags and street fighting' (whatever happened to the blood flowing in the gutters?); but it is the idea of a 'fundamental shift of power'. He still wished to transform a society in which the only relationship between a man earning £50,000 a year and a man earning fifteen shillings a week was that the former robbed the latter. What has made socialist revolution not a textbook expression but a real possibility, he says, is the war. Ever since Dunkirk the government had been taking increasing powers upon itself; socialism had become synonymous with the war effort. He described the equality of war sacrifice as 'war-communism'. In this way Orwell managed to picture the socialist revolution as, on the one hand, a clear expression of British decency, and on the other, as a political system concerned to optimise the efficient use of resources through central planning. The socialist revolution was not about destroying the family but about replacing those in control of the family fortunes. And it had already begun!

This represents a watering down of Orwell's hopes, and although it should be remembered that it was written with a clear propaganda aim in mind, it is also clear that he was beginning to recognise the radical impact that the war was having upon British society, and believed that he could reasonably expect what would amount to a revolutionary transformation later. Indeed, if we consider his six-point programme for a socialist Britain set out in this essay, we see that many of his hopes were in fact to be fulfilled: nationalisation of land, mines, railways, banks and major industries; limitation of incomes and a minimum wage; democratic reform of the education system; immediate dominion status for India and a programme for full independence; formation of a fully representative council to manage the affairs of the empire; a declaration of a formal war-time alliance with all the victims of the Axis.

It is true that they were not fulfilled in the manner that Orwell expected. He did not recognise the Attlee government as 'revolutionary', claiming dismissively that Labour candidates were generally selected for their 'political docility', with elderly trade union officials being given a seat as a 'kind of a pension'.[37] Another of his criticisms, however, had more substance; as a party of the unions Labour clearly had a direct interest in the prosperity of British capital.[38] Yet he recognised revolutionary elements within Labour. As late as mid-1942 he was expecting Cripps to 'leave the government and proclaim a revolutionary policy.'[39] (He was not alone: Borkenau, whose judgement Orwell valued, had also spoken of Britain's being in the first stage of revolution.)[40] By the following year, however, Orwell had changed his views: the opportunities of Dunkirk and Singapore had been missed.[41] Indeed, by the end of the war he had become embarrassed by his earlier expectations and predictions. Writing to *Partisan Review* he admitted having fallen into the trap of believing that 'the war and the revolution were inseparable'. He admitted to a major error of judgement, for 'after all, we have not lost the war and we have not introduced socialism'.[42] He admitted, too, that he had over-emphasised the anti-fascist nature of the war and exaggerated social changes.

By the time that he had finished *Animal Farm*, then, Orwell's thinking had undergone a major change. He had, after all, been a supporter of pacifism, writing in August 1937 that war only happened when it was in the interests of capital and that fascism was only a rival form of imperialism.[43] Any capitalist nation fighting a war against fascism would itself quickly become fascist.[44] This argument had been proved false. There was, he admitted, no British fascism and no British revolution. The democratic socialism in which he still passionately believed lived in a world of demons. If it was to survive, let alone triumph, then it had to be protected. Socialists had to be brought to understand who their enemies were, and his 'new model' of socialist revolution had to be distinguished very clearly from the old. Thus, when he wrote *Animal Farm*, Orwell was mounting an attack on Stalin's Russian revolution, in the name of decency and justice, and from a revolutionary socialist (mark two) viewpoint. While the book does not slavishly follow the events of the Russian revolution, the parallels are unmistakable. Marx, Stalin and Trotsky – and indeed the poet Mayakovsky – are clearly represented. Events such as the 1917 revolution iself, the Kronstadt naval rebellion of 1921, the Treaty of Rapollo in 1922 (which ended the Western boycott of the USSR), the German invasion of Russia, the Tehran conference of 1944, are all unmistakable. So are three definable periods in Soviet history: collectivisation (1929–33), the purges (1933–8) and the rapprochement with Germany (1939–41). In short the fable clearly represents an allegory of the Russian revolution and post-revolution.

Yet Orwell admitted to having a broader intention along the lines I have hinted at. He wrote that his aim was to show that that kind of revolution (violent, conspiratorial, led by unconsciously power-hungry people) could only result in one group of leaders replacing another. 'You can't have a revolution unless you make it for yourself, there is no such thing as a benevolent dictatorship.'[45]

For all that Orwell identified his target – the Russian revolution and those like it – it can be argued that *Animal Farm* hits not so much the Soviet bull's-eye as the sacred cow of revolution itself. It could be said that when he brought down Stalin's revolution, he brought the whole enterprise of revolution down with it, since all revolutions tend, by their nature, to be violent, conspiratorial and led by the power-hungry.

Eliot, it will be remembered, compared the work to *Gulliver's Travels*. Swift's satire was aimed at specific contemporary targets and the reader of the period would have been very well aware of who these were. Nevertheless, his statements are not bound by particular historical events and characters; they have a universal reference and can hit contemporary targets which Swift knew nothing of. Similarly, is impossible to believe that in a hundred years people will not read and learn from *Animal Farm*, though the names and events of the Russian revolution may mean very little to them. What they will learn is that revolutions tend to fail, and why.

Animal Farm is an account of a revolution on Manor Farm. This revolution occurred sometime after a speech, delivered by an old and respected boar named Major, modelled very much on the concluding section of the Communist Manifesto. Major declared that all animals are equal and all men enemies; only by continuing to eschew the customs of humankind could they maintain their condition of equality. So they must never wear clothes, live in a house, drink, smoke, use money or engage in trade. Animal society may be taken to represent humanity, and certain of the animals *are* clearly intended to be broadly representational. For example, the pigs – the cleverest of the animals – stand for the intellectuals and ideologues whom Orwell so despised; the horses, Boxer and Clover, stand for the better-off section of the working class; the sheep are the unthinking proles, like those Andalusian soldiers who did not even know which party they belonged to; the raven stands (roughly) for the church militant and Benjamin the donkey is Albert Camus' 'good witness', the dispassionate observer, in part Orwell himself.

Major set the chief task of the days ahead as being to educate all the animals for revolution, to create a true political consciousness. This task fell to the pigs, as the cleverest of the animals, with the most prominent parts being taken by Snowball, Napoleon and Squealer (i.e. Trotsky, Stalin and Mayakovsky). Major died before the revolution dawned, but dawn it duly did, and sooner than any had expected. One midsummer's eve Jones the farmer got drunk and forgot to put out food for the animals next morning. As the day wore on they became so hungry that they broke into the store shed. This roused the farmer who got his men together to drive the animals out. But the animals fought back, and so, before they realised what was happening, the rebellion had been successful. The first stage in the revolutionary agenda had been accomplished with surprising ease, and now the task at hand was to establish a revolutionary society.

The majority of the animals, says Orwell, were blissfully happy at the departure of their masters but had not the least idea of what was to become of them. 'They rolled in the dew, they cropped mouthfuls of the sweet summer grass, the kicked up clods of the black earth and smelt its rich scent.' Not the pigs. We soon see that Snowball and Napoleon have taken effective control. It is revealed that in the preceding three months the pigs had taught themselves to read and write, and they wrote on the big barn-wall the seven commandments incorporating the spirit of animalism; thereafter they set about organising the other animals. Two developments in these early days of the revolution are worth noting. First, the fate of the milk and the apples. 'Never mind the milk, comrades,' said Napoleon when asked. It was being given to the pigs for their exclusive use: so too the apples. Squealer was good enough to explain to the other animals that this was necessary because these particular foods were particularly good for brain-workers; 'This has been proved by science, comrades.' It was the pigs' *duty* to consume the milk and apples. Second, the fact that, from the beginning, the pigs did not actually work but instead directed and supervised the others. 'With their superior knowledge it was natural that they should assume the leadership.'

Orwell seems to be making a common-sense observation here: all animals are *not* equal and it is natural for the more intelligent to take control. In a revolution the traditional structure of authority is broken and a new one is needed. Naturally the intellectuals (in the absence here of the military) will take control. Is it not equally natural that they will assume some privileges? Interesting, too, that Napoleon and Snowball (Stalin and Trotksy) were quite agreed upon this. The source of the pigs' authority was superior intellect, and they soon had many schemes underway to improve productivity on the farm. By their nature, since they required various forms of expertise, these schemes were likely only to enhance the power of the pigs. So not only did the pigs master various essential technical skills but they naturally dominated the meetings of the animals; it was they who put forward all the resolutions to be voted upon.

Technological advance was the safeguard of the revolution on Animal Farm and if Snowball appreciated this first, Napoleon grasped the fact soon enough. The hoped-for better lifestyle could only be achieved through 'industrialisation' and the necessary materials could only be obtained through trade. Why had Major warned the animals against trade? Trade required producing not for need but for exchange, and whereas the former could be readily quantified the latter could not. Some animals then would be required to produce to order. The linchpin of Snowball's technological programme was to be the building of a windmill which would generate electric power, and it was against this plan that Napoleon took his stand. He offered no alternative plan to increase productivity; he raised no moral or intellectual objections to the project; he did not attack it as a threat to the principles of animalism. But when Snowball laid the plans out on the floor for the other animals to see, Napoleon urinated on them. The windmill had been Snowball's idea and not his own. This was not the only issue between the two however; Snowball wished to send pigeons to other farms encouraging animal revolt, whereas Napoleon thought it necesary to establish a *modus vivendi* with nearby farmers. What Orwell seems to be suggesting, however, is that the division within the leadership is inevitable because its base is personal rivalry, though that rivalry will deck itself out in doctrine and strategy.

It was when the animals met to decide finally on the windmill that Napoleon introduced his most persuasive argument: nine huge dogs with brass-studded collars, each trained in complete obedience to him. Snowball barely escaped with his life. Thereafter Napoleon announced the cessation of the meetings, which had been farcical anyway, in favour of a committee of pigs charged with running the farm. Stage two of the revolution had been completed: the struggle for power was over.

At this point Napoloen decided to build the windmill after all, and to engage in the necessary trade with humans. In order to build their windmill, says Orwell simply, the animals worked like slaves. The pigs meanwhile had moved into the farmhouse and were sleeping on the beds, taking care to amend the relevant commandment (for those animals who could still read) which now read that no animals should sleep on a bed *with sheets*. From now on it would seem that technological efficiency and not egalitarianism was the goal, and the leadership was beginning to assume a traditional role, taking on the traditional privileges. Yet even this efficiency proved unattainable when the windmill was blown down because its walls were too thin, and the potato harvest was lost because the clamps failed to keep out the frost.

Squealer's task was to amend the commandments as required so that the legitimacy of the regime was not in question. When the pigs began to drink alcohol the relevant commandment forbade animals to drink alcohol *to excess*. At the first sign of opposition to the pigs' rule, when the hens refused to lay the number of eggs required for trading, Napoleon acted with great brutality, and this ushered in a period of show-trials in which animals were forced to confess to crimes they most certainly did not commit (always organised by the banished Snowball). Whereas Jones the farmer had been careless of the animals' welfare and occasionally cruel, the pigs were now using terror systematically as a means of social control.

And so Animal Farm moved inexorably towards totalitarian tyranny and only occasionally does Orwell hint at possible alternatives. For example Napoleon set his dogs on Boxer the great cart-horse, who had expressed some reservations about the drift of policy. Boxer dispersed and could easily have killed the dogs but, being one of Napoleon's greatest supporters, this powerful but kindly giant did no such thing. The only hope, it seemed, lay with the proles, but their political naivety made it most unlikely that they would recognise their strength and use it.

On its own terms the revolution on Animal Farm had clearly failed. The animals were working harder than previously; they no longer believed they were working for themselves. The moral principles of animalism were slowly perverted as each proved impracticable or simply a hindrance to the pigs' aspirations. It could be argued that this failure was the result of the animals being catapulted into revolution unready – the bourgeois revolution still not completed. Yet could the most numerous of the animals, the sheep, ever have acquired political consciousness? Their only contribution to ideological consciousness was to learn to bleat in unison: 'Four legs good, two legs bad' and to change it, when the situation demanded, to 'Four legs good, two legs better'. In one of his earlier 'London letters' to *Partisan Review*, Orwell remarked on those who had been busy knitting socks for the Finns the previous year but were now busy knitting them for the Russians![46]

We would do well to remember, too, into whose tender 'hands' political education had been entrusted. As H. M. Hyndman once wrote: 'A slave class cannot free itself. The leadership, the initiative, the teaching, the organisation, must come from those comrades who are in a different position or who are trained to use their faculties in early life.'[47] It seems that in revolution there is no escape from the pigs.

It might also be argued that the revolution failed because the leadership forsook its principles and lost contact with the masses. This assumes that the pigs once did have a commitment to the principles of revolution. Even if we accept that dubious assumption, the problem remains that in the early days the only aspiration on the part of the animals had been to crop mouthfuls of the rich summer grass; they required to be organised by their natural leaders. In other words the reification of the principles of animalism was the task of a leadership unlikely to countenance the canvassing of alternatives. The control of Animal Farm had passed from a social to a political élite. The choice for the animals, as presented by Orwell, was simple enough: to be tyrannised by a drunken human or by a pig.

After the revolution comes the post-revolution; a truism, but it draws attention to the fact that a period exists after a revolutionary regime has secured itself in power when it must establish the guidelines for future social and political development. Most revolutionary writers realised that these would be hard times. William Morris, for example, referred to the masses being guided by the 'reflex of starvation', thus allowing the revolutionary government to secure obedience as it set up the community-based structure which characterised Morris's utopia. On Animal Farm the guiding principle was fear, which allowed Napoleon to mould the farm much as he chose. And what he chose undermined animalism entirely. First, he began to trade with local farms. Then the pigs discovered the attractions of the demon drink and began to sow a small paddock with barley as a result. Then came the greatest of treacheries when Boxer, that great Stakhanovite who had worked himself literally almost to death for Napoleon and Animal Farm, instead of being put out to grass, was packed off in a van to the knacker's yard. The animals shouted a warning to Boxer as the van drove off the farm, and they heard in response a tremendous drumming of hooves from inside the van, as Boxer sought unsuccessfully to kick his way out. 'There had been a time when a few kicks from Boxer's hoof would have smashed the van to matchwood.' In short, the working class has been broken and no longer poses a potential threat to the regime.

In the meantime the process of industrialisation went on apace; one windmill built, others under construction. Yet the promised electrification and all the ensuing benefits did not happen. The pigs appear to have adopted the capitalist device of mechanisation leading to increased productivity and not to shorter hours. Food had become scarcer, though Squealer's statistics proved the opposite, all forms of production on the farm having risen. All the same, Orwell remarks, there were days when the animals would 'sooner have had less figures and more food'.

It was around this time that the animals saw something which turned their world upside down. They saw Squealer walking on his hind legs carrying a whip in his trotter. By now, as Benjamin, who could still read, informed Clover, there was only one commandment on the wall of the big barn. It was to become one of the most memorable and pregnant aphorisms in modern literature:

All animals are equal
But some animals are more
Equal than others.

The final scene in the book is similarly memorable. Laughter and singing drew the animals to the farmhouse, where Napoleon and some of the pigs were playing cards with local farmers. There was a sudden violent quarrel and everybody was up and shouting. 'The creatures outside looked from pig to man, from man to pig, and from pig to man again; but already it was impossible to say which was which.'

Animal Farm has seen a complete revolution, from slavery and back full circle to slavery. The sequence of events which Orwell has pictured seems inevitable, with the post-revolution failing as ineluctably as the revolution itself had done.

It could be said that in writing *Animal Farm* Orwell exposed the hollowness of his own optimism, for it is difficult to see the story as merely a satire on the Russian revolution alone: as I have suggested, it is a paradigm for all revolutions. In an article written in 1944, Orwell chides Arthur Koestler because he seems to believe that revolutionaries seek to create a utopia but in fact

perhaps the choice before man is always a choice of evils, perhaps even the aim of socialism is not to make the world perfect but to make it better. All revolutions are failures, but they are not all the same failure. [34]

Such epigrammatic observations beg as many questions as they answer. Both Koestler and Orwell were acute observers of human nature, and both instruct us that mankind, shorn of customs and familiar structures, frequently finds itself at a loss. The stupendous difficulty of organising a revolution in a modern state, or attempting to pick up the pieces after a spontaneous revolt, must not be forgotten. Writing of the prospects for a socialist revolution at the end of the last century, Bernard Shaw remarked that to carry off a revolution when there were only fourteen prisoners in the Bastille was one thing; to do so when there were forty million was quite another. The supreme paradox of the revolution, moreover, as *Animal Farm* – and indeed Koestler's *Darkness at Noon* and *The Gladiators* – show us, is that without a political consciousness there can be no successful revolution and without a successful revolution there can be no political consciousness. When Orwell worked on this outstanding book in those years of war, he must have known this in his heart; Napoleon the pig certainly did.

5 The politics of ideology

Orwell had been a well-known and respected figure in literary circles for some time, and the publication of *Animal Farm* made him something of a public figure too, though fame hardly exploded upon him like one of George Bowling's frankfurters in *Coming Up for Air*. Nevertheless, his celebrity prompted a number of people to request his support for worthy causes, so that he became more active in the public domain while maintaining his relentless drive to write. For example, he actively involved himself in the protest against the harrying of British anarchists and pacifists, while making it plain that his support did not imply acceptance of their views. He denounced with some passion a Special Branch raid on the offices of the anarchist publication *War Commentary* in 1944, and later attacked in *Tribune* the sentencing of its editors to nine months in prison for attempting to 'undermine the affections' of members of the armed forces.

Believing that the National Council for Civil Liberties had become largely a communist front interested chiefly in protecting its supporters and fellow-travellers, Orwell become vice-chairman of the alternative Freedom Defence Committee, a group comprising a number of notable figures, such as E. M. Forster, Augustus John, Benjamin Britten and Osbert Sitwell, the aim of which were 'to uphold the essential liberty of individuals and organisations, and to defend those who are persecuted for exercising their rights to freedom of speech, writing and action'.¹ Typically he took his responsibilities very seriously. Equally typically he found the focus of the committee, predominantly defending left-wingers against political prosecutions, too narrow and, along with Koestler, Bertrand Russell and Victor Gollancz, attempted to establish a League for the Dignity and Rights of Man. He drafted the aims and objectives of such a league, which were to further equal opportunities, to protect against economic exploitation and to champion freedom of expression. These aims and objectives were to be secured by the establishment of a journal and by lobbying in support of

political prisoners and against oppressive laws everywhere. The similarity of these objectives with those of Amnesty International is striking, but the attempt to establish the League was aborted when the
prime backer decided to invest his money in an entirely different
enterprise – nightclub revue.[2] Other requests came his way, but by
this time Orwell had decided to concentrate his energies: 'Everyone
keeps coming at me, wanting me to lecture, to write commissioned
booklets, to join this and that, etc. – you don't know how much I pine
to get free of it all and have time to think again.'[3]

'Thinking again' involved not merely time for reflection but also
organising regular lunches with a number of literary figures including
Malcolm Muggeridge, Anthony Powell, and Julian Symons. It could
have done Orwell no harm to have traded ideas with such astute people
but lonely though he was he never permitted these meetings to inter-
fere with his well-disciplined work pattern.

Another matter which took up his time was the battle to make
proper domestic arrangements for the care of his son. Mutual friends
introduced him to Susan Watson, a recently separated mother of a
seven-year-old child, who was to care for both Richard and George for
about a year. She found Orwell by no means an easy man to live with, 'a
conflicting mixture of emotional inhibition and intellectual expan-
siveness'. His dietary requirements were idiosyncratic (everything had
to be 'just so') and the daily routine was quite rigid. He would work
till 3 a.m. and then sleep until 7.45 a.m. when he was to be awakened
gently, since he suffered badly from nightmares. If there was something almost ritualistic about Orwell's existence in these days, it probably was as much a consequence of the need to keep melancholia at bay
as a manifestation of his innate fastidiousness.

According to Susan Watson, life was interesting rather than eventful
at this time, although in February 1946 he had another haemorrhage
which kept him in bed for two weeks, though he did not seek medical
advice. In May of that year Orwell's older sister Marjorie died at the
age of forty-eight of a kidney disease, and naturally he went up for the
funeral, setting off alone afterwards for Jura. Avril, his younger sister,
followed him a week later.

There is an almost perverse predictability about much of what
Orwell did in his life. Perhaps there were worse ideas for a tubercular
single parent than moving to an abandoned farmhouse five miles from
the nearest made-up road at the far end of one of the wetter of the

Hebridean islands, but surely not many. Only Orwell could have com-pounded this by buying from his old comrade from Spain, Georges Kopp, who had a farm in Midlothian, a van that was in an even worse physical condition than Orwell himself. Crick sees sense in Orwell's plan – a well-considered one, we must remember – to get away from it all, and points quite correctly to the relative mildness of the Hebridean climate. But the climate was damp and Orwell was a sick man with no propensity to become a hermit. 'Getting away from it all' in the home counties is one thing; in the Hebrides it is quite another. Richard Rees' opinion was clearly enough voiced: Orwell had 'contrived to find the most uninhabitable house in the British Isles'. To a consider-able degree the move was a typical thumbing of the Orwellian nose at the Fates.

If Barnhill was a remote place to live, it was a charming spot to visit in the summer and Orwell was not to be short of summertime visitors. Not all of them got on very well with Avril. In fact, during his first stay on the island, his housekeeper Susan Watson was another who found Avril somewhat prickly and intolerant. Orwell tended to withdraw to his study-bedroom to avoid the domestic turmoil. As a consequence he actually began to work on his final novel sooner than he had intended, though not at that time with any apparent sense of urgency. Neverthe-less, having already decided that this summer was primarily to be a holiday, his days were largely taken up with sorting out his vegetable garden, fishing and shooting and so on, and if he was aware of the growing struggle between his sister and his housekeeper he took no sides. Having lost her parents and her sister, Avril had clearly decided to devote her energies to caring for her brother and nephew, and she did not approve of Susan's established practices. Things came to a head and Susan appealed to Orwell. Although sympathetic to her point of view he made it clear that he would not ask his sister to leave. The matter was finally settled when, with Orwell's agreement, Susan invited a friend, who was a communist, to stay. Though he was warned to keep off politics, he and Orwell clashed, and Susan and her friend clashed with Avril. Both left Barnhill after a violent argument with the latter, and although Richard is said to have been extremely upset at losing Susan, her departure had little effect on Orwell.

At about this time Orwell's van finally arrived from Midlothian. Such was its condition that it could not be driven off the ferry but had to be lifted off manually. It was to be abandoned on the spot where it was landed, where it stood for a long time to come as a rusting monument to Spanish comradeship.

In the autumn the family returned to London, and with Avril now performing the domestic duties, Orwell slipped into his old routine of inviting friends round for high tea. Another routine into which he was soon to slip was writing his old weekly *Tribune* column 'As I Please'. He offered to write a lengthy critique of the Attlee government for *Tribune*, but was dissuaded from doing so. He was generally somewhat disillusioned by the government's failure to bring in some symbolically important reforms, such as the abolition of private education and the House of Lords. Much of his writing during the winter comprised correspondence and articles. He clearly intended to leave his novel until the following summer at Jura, though his articles indicate that his attention was focusing increasingly on the issues which he was to raise in *Nineteen Eighty-four*.

In April 1947, after another winter of bronchitis, the family journeyed north to Jura again, though Orwell in fact had made a flying visit in the middle of winter to plant some fruit trees. Soon after arriving he wrote to Sonia Brownwell warmly inviting her to visit, though she declined and discouraged any thought of a second invitation. A new neighbour had arrived on Jura, an ex-army officer named Bill Dunn, and he and the Orwells began to see quite a lot of each other. Soon enough Orwell had got back to work on his novel and he was able to report to Warburg that he hoped to have the first draft finished by October, health permitting. But he spoke ominously of being slowed down by wretched health and this was clearly a factor that was playing on his mind. He wrote later to Anthony Powell about a 'limited capacity for work nowadays' which needed to be carefully husbanded.[4] He was finding the novel a difficult proposition because it was 'in a sense, a fantasy, but in the form of a naturalistic novel'. Under separate cover Orwell also sent the typescript of *Such, Such Were the Joys*, which he hoped to see printed 'sooner or later when the people most concerned are dead'.[5] In fact, although one version of the essay appeared in America in the 1950s, British publication did not occur until some months after the death of Mrs Wilkes in 1968. There has been some debate about the timing of *Such*, because some critics, especially Anthony West,[6] have argued that *Nineteen Eighty-four* should be read primarily as a flight of sado-masochistic imagination based upon Orwell's experiences at school. This theory would clearly be somewhat strengthened had Orwell been working on both at the same time. There is no evidence to support this however: indeed Orwell's letter to Warburg makes apologetic reference to the condition of the corrected typescript and it seems probable that the original had been in his possession for some time. Moreover, as Crick points out,[7] even in the unlikely event of both having been written at the same time, there is no good reason to suppose that *Such* was the 'influencer' and not the 'influenced'. More important, surely, is the certain fact that the main themes of *Nineteen Eighty-four* had been planned for some time, and were anyway incomparably broader in conceptual sweep than the themes of the autobiographical sketch.

In his letter to Warburg, Orwell also made reference to Richard's cutting his head open. It took a journey and wait of six hours before the wound could be stitched. If he needed further evidence of the risk he was taking with his health by living in such an isolated spot, this was surely it.

Though a number of visitors came up that summer, including his brother-in-law Humphrey Dakin and his children, Orwell spent most of the time working. However, he did find time almost to kill himself, along with his niece, Dakin and Richard when he attempted to navigate the waters of Coirevrechan, the infamous whirlpool and tidal race, and they were nearly drowned.

Towards the end of the summer Orwell was once again in poor health, and was obliged to finish work on the first draft of his new novel while in bed. By the end of October it was done, and he took to his bed completely exhausted. By December he was running a temperature and returning to London was out of the question. He sent for a chest specialist, who made the trip out to Barnhill and recommended a stay in a sanatorium. Just before Christmas 1947 Orwell left Barnhill, where the snowdrops were out and some tulips beginning to show, for Hairmyres Hospital in East Kilbride.

Orwell spent seven months at Hairmyres and endured a long and painful course of treatment which made serious revision work on *Nineteen Eighty-four* out of the question. However he was able to do some reviewing, which brought in much-needed money. He wrote to Warburg that if he was able to leave Hairmyres by June he would finish the novel by the end of the year. Although Crick remains adamant that Orwell's schedule was not prompted by fear of death, it would have been odd indeed if the possibility had not acted as a spur. His letter to

Warburg indicates Orwell's state of mind concerning the book and his health clearly enough: 'It's a ghastly mess as it stands, but the idea is so good that I could not possibly abandon it. If anything should happen to me I've instructed Richard Rees, my literary executor, to destroy the ms without showing it to anybody . . . .'[8]

Orwell's hopes of a recovery were pinned upon a new drug, streptomycin, which had been used to great effect in treating tuberculosis in the United States, but was too expensive to be readily available in the United Kingdom. Orwell was able to prevail upon his friend David Astor to obtain the drug from contacts in America. He began treatment in March and at first the results were most encouraging. However, he soon began to suffer acute side-effects, and after fifty days the treatment was discontinued. Orwell described these side-effects with harrowing detachment in his notebook, and it is easy to see what formed the basis for the description of the physical deterioration under torture of Winston Smith. Despite this great set-back, Orwell's condition had improved sufficiently for him to return to Jura towards the end of July 1948. He was ordered to 'take things very quietly for a long time, perhaps a year or so', and spend only six hours or so out of bed each day.[9] Orwell was to spend six weeks of excellent summer weather on the island, staying in bed for about half of the day, spending much time playing with Richard, and working. Avril kept friends from visiting Barnhill by fair means or foul – though not always successfully – and the house was far more relaxed than previously, partly because Avril herself had struck up a relationship with Bill Dunn who, by this time, had charge of farming Barnhill. Orwell managed to type in bed or laid out on a sofa without too much difficulty, and planned to finish revising the typescript by early November, though towards the end he hit a difficulty. As he had earlier admitted, the first draft was a 'ghastly mess', and his revisions were profuse: he really needed the services of a professional typist to help him cope with the final draft. He set about acquiring one, having finally completed his revisions, but those to whom he turned were unable to help him and he finally had to retype the whole book himself. With typical understatement he wrote to his agent that 'it really wasn't worth all this fuss. It's merely that as it tires me to sit upright for any length of time I can't type very neatly and can't do many pages a day.'[10] In fact, the typing brought Orwell very close to a total physical collapse.

In early December, however, the typescript was in the post to

Warburg and Orwell was at once exhausted and relieved, but frustrated that the execution of the idea had not been better done – he was later to write to Julian Symons that he had 'ballsed it up rather'.[11] His health was by now so bad that he knew he needed to go to a sanatorium urgently and just before Christmas 1948 he left a bitterly cold Jura for the last time. Even his departure was to prove traumatic, the car getting stuck in a pothole and Orwell having to stay in the freezing vehicle with Richard while Avril and Bill Dunn walked four miles for help. He travelled straight down to Cranham, a private sanatorium in the Cotswolds.

For several months there was little change in his condition; various treatments were tried, but to no great effect. Many friends and notables came to see him, including the socialist historian R. H. Tawney, and he was generally more comfortable in the private institution than he had been in Hairmyres, well though he had been treated there. Typically, he observed in his notebook his reaction during visiting to hearing so many more upper-class English accents than he had grown accustomed to over recent years: 'And what voices! A sort of over-fedness, a fatuous self-confidence, a constant bah-bahing of laughter about nothing, above all, a . . . fundamental ill-will – people who, one instinctively feels, without ever being able to see them, are the enemies of anything intelligent or sensitive or beautiful. No wonder everyone hates us so.' (Orwell had lost none of his pungency as a social critic.)[12] One pleasant surprise, however, was a letter from his old childhood sweetheart Jacintha Buddicom, who had only recently discovered his identity, to which he sent two letters in reply.

The medical prognosis for Orwell was that recovery to the point of being permanently in a wheelchair was quite possible, but Warburg, Astor and others had decided upon a second opinion. As Orwell himself had written to Warburg, even if nothing could be done for him, he wanted to know how long he was likely to live. A consultant at University College Hospital in London, who had treated D. H. Lawrence during his last illness, was approached. His view was that if Orwell desisted from serious writing for several months then he might attain a condition of 'the good chronic' – i.e. able to 'potter about and do a few hours' sedentary work'.[13] It was of some considerable comfort to Orwell himself to know what his prospects were and, on the whole, they were probably at least as good as he might have hoped, though the next few months would be crucial. Indeed, in late summer he suffered a slight relapse and soon after was transferred to University College Hospital in London.

Meanwhile other developments had been taking place in his life. In the spring of 1949 Orwell had received a visit from Sonia Brownwell. Since their brief affair, so unsatisfactory from her point of view, Orwell had attained considerable celebrity and she had always been attracted to famous men of letters. Moreover, an affair with Merleau-Ponty had just been ended by him with some acrimony, and so she did not reject Orwell's second proposal of marriage.

In August Orwell informed Warburg that he intended to marry and soon after his arrival in London he broke the news to David Astor, explaining that, to his surprise, friends, relatives and medical advisers had thought the marriage a good idea. Sonia herself had argued that, if she were his wife, there would be no problems about their travelling together in the likely event of his eventually transferring to a sanatorium overseas. Almost immediately she began to busy herself with his affairs, taking off his shoulders much of the routine secretarial work, and for a brief period Orwell enjoyed a detachment and indeed a pale optimism.

The marriage took place on October 13 1949, after David Astor had obtained a special licence from the Archbishop of Canterbury. Orwell was forty-six years old and Sonia thirty-one. Though married from his bed, he dressed in some style. After the brief ceremony David Astor took the party for a wedding lunch at the Ritz and brought back a copy of the menu, signed by them all, to Orwell.

The plan now was to travel to a sanatorium in Switzerland, and a plane was chartered for late January for the journey. A few days before, as a precaution, he made out a new will in which Sonia was to be the sole beneficiary, though an insurance policy was set up to provide for Richard's education. Strangely, no provision was made for Avril. The document concluded with the direction that he was to be buried according to the rites of the Church of England. Those of his friends and family who could, visited him during the last day or two before his flight. Malcolm Muggeridge noticed a fishing rod at the foot of the bed; no doubt an assault on some Swiss mountain stream was being planned. However on the night of January 21 1950 Orwell suffered a haemorrhage and died soon afterwards. Sonia could not be contacted as she had gone to a nightclub with the artist Lucien Freud (a former lover), who had helped her organise the flight to Switzerland, and a female friend.

David Astor had one final favour to perform for his friend, and found him a plot in the grounds of the beautiful country church of All Saints at Sutton Courtenay, Berkshire, where he was buried after a quiet funeral service. Orwell's son Richard continued to live with Avril, who married Bill Dunn in 1951 and moved from Barnhill to the mainland. Two months after her husband's death, Sonia took a long holiday in the South of France, where Merleau-Ponty joined her, though once again the relationship foundered, this time permanently. Sonia remained committed to promoting Orwell's work, and was partly instrumental in publishing the collection of his essays and journals in 1968. She died in 1980 at the age of sixty-two.

Although there has been some debate on the subject, Crick's authoritative biography is convincingly clear that Orwell did not see *Nineteen Eighty-four* as his last novel. He hoped and rather expected to live. On the other hand, we have already considered equally clear evidence that he was quite sanguine about his prospects, and that he must have known that in working so hard to finish the book he could be shortening his life drastically. The facts suggest that he may well have sacrificed himself for the book. George Woodcock saw the book as 'the culmination of twenty years of writing, and an authentic product, not of the tortured body registered at various sanatoria under the name of Eric Blair, but of the imaginative being who bore the name of George Orwell.'[14]

A number of books had influenced Orwell's thinking, and he made no secret of the fact. Indeed, in a review article entitled 'James Burnham and the Managerial Revolution'[15] he discusses the chief themes of several books from which he drew inspiration. They were: Burnham's *The Managerial Revolution* and *The Machiavellians*, Huxley's *Brave New World* and Zamyatin's *We* (which he thought particularly highly of because it identified the reality of 'cruelty as an end in itself'). In his review of Eugene Lyons' *Assignment in Utopia*, Orwell observes that many of the theories discussed by Burnham and others had actually been put into practice in the USSR during the 1930s.[16] Burnham's writing was principally concerned with the problem of groups attempting to gain power by cynically manipulating an ideology – the British Puritans, the French Jacobins and the Russian Bolsheviks being good examples. The aim of all such groups is to enjoy power and its privileges (though Burnham considered that they would be cynical enough to realise that it would be easier to do so if they *appeared* to serve the

common good). Orwell was seized by the idea that politics represented a specialised aspect of human behaviour, identified by complete
unscrupulousness, which was of interest only to small groups within
society; the great majority were apathetic and apolitical. Thus power
could never be restrained by ethical or religious codes requiring the
sanction of a majority but only by other power holders. Burnham, said
Orwell, was exposing the wish of the British Russophile intelligentsia
to destroy egalitarian socialism and replace it with a 'hierarchical
society where the intellectual can at last get his hands on the whip'.
But Orwell believed that Burnham had failed to explain *why* the intellectuals wanted power; he himself would do so at some length, and the
idea of the whip would be central.

Although it is widely recognised that Orwell's Spanish experiences
led him to question the integrity of some left-wing intellectuals,
especially communists and fellow-travellers, it should be remembered
that his battle with the intellectuals was of older origins. In his Eton
days, it will be recalled, he was spoken of as liking to present himself as
the 'new Bernard Shaw' and we are told that he had read all of the
works of Shaw and H. G. Wells. They were his heroes and they were
socialists. They were also intellectuals.

History has written a part for the Fabians as benevolent ladies and
gentlemen whose great achievement was to moderate and make respectable the Edwardian socialist movement. There is, in fact, a pronounced disparity between the Fabian myth and its reality. Critics like
Leonard Woolf,[17] who have helped to propagate the 'drawing-room
socialist-myth of respectability and moderation can have read little
history, beyond that written by Fabians. Their major polemicists, such
as Shaw, the Webbs and Wells, were not democrats in the normal
sense of the word. Indeed their temper was highly élitist. It was the
Fabians, after all, who set up the London School of Economic and
Political Science (LSE) precisely to produce the well-trained élite that
would, like some modern class of Platonic guardians, rule in the
interests of all. 'Socialism without experts,' said Shaw, 'is as impossible as . . . dentistry without experts'.[18] And we should not misunder-
stand Shaw, who once declared himself to be a national socialist before
Hitler was born;[19] his heroes and heroines are for the most part men
and women of action who command and expect to be obeyed, and his
definition of democracy: 'a social order aiming at the greatest available
welfare for the whole population'. Socialism was not about giving

power to the people. No Fabian would do that, said Shaw unless 'his real objective were to achieve a *reductio ad absurdum* of democracy and have done with it forever'.[20] So for the Fabians socialism was a kind of castor oil to be forced between the teeth of a reluctant working class by a kind and intelligent middle-class health visitor. Small wonder that Shaw and a number of leading Fabians were strong supporters of Stalin and of Soviet communism. When Orwell identified these socialist intellectuals as his enemies, he was not being paranoid.

I have said that Orwell also believed that totalitarianism was at root not a political system but a state of mind. This is a theme which dominated a lot of his writing during the early war years but perhaps is most clearly set out in a piece which I should like to examine in a little detail, written for *Horizon* in October of 1944 and entitled 'Raffles and Miss Blandish'. In this essay Orwell compares two crime stories, one from 1900 and one from 1939. Raffles, the hero of the first, is a burglar but he is also a gentleman and has represented his country at cricket. On the rare occasions that Raffles expresses remorse, it is 'almost purely social; he has disgraced ''his old school'', he has lost his right to enter ''decent society'', he has forfeited his amateur status and become a cad.' Within this value system certain things are 'not done', Raffles will not abuse hospitality, regards friendship as sacred, acts chivalrously towards women and is intensely patriotic. Raffles' world is entirely governed by this morality, a morality which, as Orwell points out, may be rather absurd but has the advantage that everybody accepts it.

Orwell moves on to discuss *No Orchids for Miss Blandish* with the simple warning: 'Now for a header into the cesspool.' The story concerns the kidnapping of Miss Blandish, a millionaire's daughter, by a gang which is then killed off by better-organised gang. They intend to murder Miss Blandish after the payment of a ransom but the brains behind the gang, a woman, sees Miss Blandish as an opportunity to cure her son of his impotence by encouraging him to rape the prisoner. This rape is finally achieved, followed by the flogging of the heroine with a rubber hosepipe. In the meantime Blandish, the father, has engaged private detectives and, through means of bribery and torture, the police are able to surprise and massacre the whole gang – except the son who escapes with Miss Blandish and manages a final rape before he too is killed. Rather than be restored to the bosom of the family, however, Miss Blandish jumps to her death. Now, Orwell's analysis shows that the novel contains eight major murders, innumerable casual killings and woundings, an exhumation, rapes, flogging, torture, a stripper, and much else (including a gangster who has an orgasm at the moment of being knifed). It takes corruption and self-seeking entirely for granted. 'Ultimately [and hence the story's importance for Orwell] only one motive is at work throughout the whole story: the pursuit of power.' And power is measured by the capacity to inflict pain; this is how the strong triumph over the weak. This relationship is symbolised by an incident which Orwell quotes from another book by the same author, in which the hero is described as stamping on somebody's face, after which, having crushed the man's mouth, he ground his heel round and round. Orwell remarks of the book that several friends had called it 'pure fascism' and he agrees, for though it has no direct connection with politics it has 'the same relationship with fascism as, say, Trollope's novels have to nineteenth-century capitalism. It is a day-dream appropriate to a totalitarian age,' which recognises no value beyond the equation of right with might.

Orwell's theme, wrote Gollo Mann, is that 'totalitarian danger lies within ourselves and in all the political systems of our time'.[21] But towards the end of the No Orchids essay, Orwell went a stage further in specifically associating British intellectual socialists with the desire for power just as he had described it here. There is an interconnection, he argued, between sadism, nationalism, success worship and totalitarianism. 'I believe no one has ever pointed out the sadistic element in Bernard Shaw's work, still less suggested that this probably has some connection with Shaw's admiration for dictators.' Countless British intellectuals, says Orwell, who 'kiss the arse' of Stalin are no different from those who gave allegiance to Hitler and Mussolini, nor indeed to Carlyle, Creasy and others in the nineteenth century who so admired the achievements of Prussianism. Orwell was anxious to establish that this cult of power tends to be mixed up with a love of cruelty for its own sake. He concluded that the English-language tradition of heroes fighting against the odds was now out of date, and Jack the Giant Killer ought to be renamed Jack the Dwarf Killer. Did Orwell know that Bernard Shaw had indeed suggested what he thought was a more appropriate theme for a modern nursery fable: Giant the Jack Killer? Orwell had, in fact, long been concerned with the propensity for 'vicarious bullying' of intellectuals, who he wrote in 1931, tended to believe in 'some vast world-purpose, unquestionably good, and that great men (meaning *successful* men) are its instruments'.[22] It is also clear from other things that he wrote that Orwell had come to dislike Shaw especially. (See letter to Brenda Salkeld.)[23] Intellectuals were bullies, then, and intellectual socialists among the worst.

If Orwell wanted to get this message across to socialists generally it was no wonder that he attracted the opprobrium of a number of socialist intellectuals: indeed *Nineteen Eighty-four* was reviewed in one communist journal under the heading 'Maggot of the month', and the reaction of the radical student in Saul Bellow's *Mr Sammler's Planet* indicates that he had not been forgiven more than twenty years later. 'Orwell was a fink,' he says. 'He was a sick counter-revolutionary. It was good he died when he did.' Even such a perceptive critic as the socialist intellectual Raymond Williams could not forgive Orwell's attacking totalitarianism through the example of *socialist* totalitarianism (or indeed revolution through the example of a socialist revolution).[24] It would have been easy enough for Orwell to have avoided these charges had he wanted to, but the point is precisely that he was writing to praise and not to bury socialism! His readers, or more correctly those for whom he was writing, did not need to be told that fascism was by its nature totalitarian; had not a world war just been fought for this very reason? They did not need to be told that many foreign regimes with an authoritarian disposition could easily slip into totalitarian ways; had not pre-war history shown that all too clearly? But what the insular British left *did* need to be told was that totalitarianism could be built by a socialist regime and that even Britain, with its long and distinguished tradition of liberal values, could provide the home for a totalitarian polity. Orwell wrote *Nineteen Eighty-four* within the British socialist tradition to warn fellow socialists to be on their guard against an intellectual élite which he despised and which he believed to be chiefly interested in power for its own sake.

The ruling class in *Nineteen Eighty-four* established itself in Oceania as the consequence of a socialist revolution and it founded a socialist state which presented itself as an organic whole, subsuming the individual interests of all. But this organicism is soon exposed, for society is organised, indeed regimented, solely for the purpose of maximising the self-interest of the ruling group. It is a perversion of Plato's republic, with power (as defined in *Miss Blandish*) and not virtue as the rulers' reward. Technology, applied specifically to the science of scrutiny, provides the means for the group's dominance, but the superstructure which it supports assigns a social role to groups with a rigidity unimaginable even in feudal Christendom. Thus Oceanic society comprises 300 million of whom party members make up 45 million (fifteen per cent); of these, six million (two per cent of the whole) belong to the Inner Party and thirty-nine million (the remaining thirteen per cent) to the Outer Party. The eighty-five per cent of the population who do not belong to the Party comprise the proletariat and are not, in the classical sense, citizens of the state at all.

The purpose of this rigid hierarchy is not immediately apparent and the novel's hero, Winston Smith, wrote in his diary that although he understood *how* the Inner Party retained its control of the state he did not understand *why*; it was clearly no longer motivated by socialist ideology. The purpose of the hierarchy was finally explained to Winston by his interrogator O'Brien as being simple – power. O'Brien defines power not as a means to obtain some end (equality or justice for example) but an end in itself. He argues that no group ever seizes power with the intention of giving it up later. Dictatorships are not set up in order to defend the revolution; rather the revolution is organised to set up a dictatorship. Power is not a means, it is an end. [25] O'Brien goes on to define power: power is being exercised when one individual forces his or her own view of reality upon another, and in a most specific way. [26]

> 'How does one man assert his power over another Winston?'
> Winston thought. 'By making him suffer', he said.
> 'Exactly. By making him suffer. Obedience is not enough. Unless he is suffering, how can you be sure that he is obeying your will and not his own? Power is in inflicting pain and humiliation. Power is in tearing human minds to pieces and putting them together again in shapes of your own choosing.'

The future, O'Brien explains to Winston, consists of the members of the Inner Party maximising power through their relationship with the Outer Party. 'If you want a picture of the future,' says O'Brien, borrowing from James Hadley Chase, 'imagine a boot stamping on a human face forever.'

This constitutes a theory of power as psychosis, arguing that those who seek political power do so simply to inflict suffering on others. Moreover in order to maximise the satisfaction which the exercise of power brings, it has to be exercised directly. On this basis a playground bully might be said to exercise greater power than a president of the United States, since the satisfactions of inflicting suffering are more immediate and direct. Can it seriously be maintained that the majority who have sought and exercised power throughout history have been motivated by no considerations other than stamping on faces? George Kateb feels that Orwell's linking of power with sadism is unsound and diminishes the strength of his warning.[27] Hannah Arendt[28] has emphasised that all ideological thinking contains elements of totalitarianism because, by definition, they provide total explanations of 'the truth'. Moreover, since totalitarian leaders declare the nature of ideology *ex cathedra*, ideology may be cynically used to sanction the pursuit of total power. This is precisely the argument that Burnham advances in *The Machiavellians* and, indeed, is similar to Popper's thesis that ideology is a means and not an end.[29] It would seem, then, that Orwell is in very good company when he links ideology with power, but not when he links both to sadism.

Perhaps what Orwell had in mind was to parody power; to show us that those who wish to create power structures, especially of a totalitarian nature, in order to create a better world for all, such as the Fabians, were concerned just as much with forcing their reality upon others, concerned just as much with creating, using and benefiting from that power structure, which they would be unwilling ever to dismantle. Isaac Deutscher argued that Orwell's 'ferocious imagination', because it lacks the subtleness and originality of the greatest satirists, leads him to overstate his case. Nevertheless his analysis is both penetrating and arresting.[30]

It would probably suit Orwell's purpose well enough if he could frighten us into understanding two things: that power is an end just as much as a means and that totalitarianism is not rational. Ironically it was the one-time Fabian H. G. Wells himself who warned against allowing a man to appoint himself as your shepherd, for sooner or later you would find a crook around your ankle. As for the second, Orwell clearly regarded it as important to explore the associated myth of totalitarian rationality. He criticises H. G. Wells for depicting history as a struggle between science and planning on the one hand and disorderly reaction on the other. The truth of the matter was quite a different thing: 'The order, the planning, the state encouragement of science, the steel, the concrete, the aeroplanes, all are there, but all in the service of ideas appropriate to the Stone Age. Science is fighting on the side of superstition.'³¹ Again, power, shown to be atavistic and irrational, is the *end*, and scientific rationality only a *means*.

The new social order of Oceania in which all pretence is stripped away allows the Inner Party to maximise power, its sadistic satisfaction gained through the suffering of others. Orwell wrote that former civilisations claimed to be founded on love or justice; the Party's order is founded on hatred. In both the old classical theories of the state and that of Oceania, private property and family life have been abolished so that nothing may come between the guardian (Inner Party member) and the state; in Oceania, moreover, all forms of passion not channelled through – indeed directed by – the state are illegal. Orwell says that family life will cease to exist at all in the future, just as in Huxley's *Brave New World*. But whereas with Huxley the power of the sex is diffused, with Orwell it is eradicated: 'We shall abolish the orgasm . . . there will be no loyalty except loyalty to the party.'³²

It was against this ruling group that Winston pitched himself. He had come to regard himself as the guardian of human values and he sought to maintain these values while recognising from the beginning the inevitability of his eventual defeat. Winston acted against the state by trying to create a private realm – through purchasing and keeping a diary and by indulging in a love affair. He also declared his willingness to act against the state politically. When O'Brien, posing as a leader of the clandestine rebels, the Brotherhood, asked Winston what acts he would be prepared to undertake against the state, Winston agreed to do anything, however devastating its effects upon innocent people. A more crucial point, however, is that Winston's treachery predated this declaration of intent, predated even the purchase of the diary; to question the infallibility of the state within the confines of one's skull was to be doomed – thoughtcrime was treachery. In much the same way that Koestler's Rubashov, in *Darkness at Noon*, nightly expected a visit from the secret police once he began to question the propriety of Number One's policies within the privacy of his own skull, so too Winston knew where his thoughtcrimes would inevitably lead. This lack of a distinction between a private and a public realm is precisely what gives life in Oceania its nightmare quality. Nobody has recourse to a private world in which he or she may regain self-esteem or attempt to control even the smallest part of their own destiny; there is no escape from Big Brother.

What are the elements of the private realm, denied by the Oceanian state, which allow an individual to be fully human? First, the right to be one's own judge of external reality, to be what Arendt calls a 'moral man'.[33] In essence it was what Martin Luther sought to establish by claiming to have direct access, as it were, to God, and not to require the mediation of the Church. The Party stands firmly against this claim, demanding that the individual be willing to reject the evidence of his or her own senses. Reality is not external, says O'Brien. It is the creation of the human mind. Not the individual mind, which makes mistakes and is mortal, but in the mind of the Party, which is collective and immortal. Whatever the Party holds to be truth *is* truth. It is impossible to see reality except by looking through the eyes of the party. It was also impossible to guess what the party might declare to be reality at some time in the future. Winston conjectures that in the end the Party would declare that two plus two made five and the individual would be required to *believe* it (to *accept* it would not be sufficient). 'It was inevitable that they should make that claim sooner or later: the logic of their position demanded it.' Indeed, when reviewing Bertrand Russell's *Power: A New Social Analysis* in 1939, Orwell had predicted an age 'in which two and two will make five when the Leader says so'.[34] Orwell drew his inspiration here from Eugene Lyons who, when writing about his experiences in the Soviet Union, had noted that when the targets of Five Year Plans were allegedly achieved in four years, adverts were put up in neon in Moscow reading: '$2 + 2 = 5$'. For Lyons these signs, with what Steinhof calls their mystical simplicity, defiance of logic and 'nose-thumbing arithmetic' came to epitomise the Soviet system.[35] For his part Winston was brought to such a poor condition physically that he was genuinely no longer certain whether, when O'Brien added two fingers to two, he could see four or five. It is important to appreciate what it is that Winston is claiming: that 'the truth' constitutes an objective reality which is accessible to the undeceived intelligence on the basis presumably of sensory witness.

Can we be confident that the sensory perception of the undeceived intelligence will always recognise the contours of objective truth? Most 'truths' are more complex and ambiguous than this simple arithmetical statement and far less amenable to sensory confirmation. Even some of the keenest minds of his day gave up the struggle to recognise the truth. Orwell had little sympathy with those of his contemporaries who joined either the Communist Party or the Roman Catholic Church because these institutions were said to provide believers with a comprehensive creed, a revealed truth,[36] which allowed little room for doubt.

For Dostoevsky the certainty that two plus two equals four was not symbolic of individual liberty, in fact quite the reverse. As one speaker declares, 'after all, gentlemen, twice two is four is not life, gentlemen, but the beginning of death . . . man has always feared this $2 \times 2 = 4$ formula and I still fear it'. It might do for ants, but not for men. 'I agree that two and two makes four is an excellent thing; but to give everything its due two and two makes five is also a very fine thing.' If working-class values were to provide a touchstone, then one of Orwell's own observations gives food for thought: he quotes a working-class mother, a 'toby-jug' figure with a very broad accent (the very kind Orwell claimed to admire) who 'adds up twenty-seven and ten and makes it thirty-one'.[37] Perception and reality are not always so closely related as all that! When Winston confronts O'Brien with his own moral selfhood, it is a moral selfhood limited to reason only, because he cannot believe in a God beyond reason or any other form of knowledge beyond that authenticated by sensory perception. Indeed Orwell was aware of these limitations. He once told an instructive story of Sir Walter Raleigh, imprisoned in the Tower and occupying himself with writing a history of the world. Sometime after completing the first volume a scuffle broke out under his window between two workmen, one of whom was killed. Despite having seen the incident and having set in train the most diligent enquiries, he was unable to unravel the true nature of the quarrel. Raleigh burned his history book. He was wrong, Orwell concluded: it *was* possible to arrive at 'the truth'.[38] In fact, though Orwell recognised that human intelligence and sensory perception frequently led down a blind alley, he was more concerned about the power relationship between the institution and the individual than about the limitations and deficiencies of human rational processes. 'He clings to a dualism of fact and value' said Patrick Reilly, as the key to that relationship.[39]

Not only was the citizen of Oceania deprived of an autonomous moral status, but also of legal status. There is no law in the state beyond the arbitrary dictates of Big Brother. There are no individual rights whatsoever. 'The State is the Law, the moral law as well as the juridical law. Thus it cannot be subject to any standard, and especially not to the yardstick of civil morality.'[40] But the totalitarian state, according to Arendt, is 'shapeless' and unpredictable.[41] Indeed the state could manipulate reality, even the past. Orwell's Spanish experiences had made him painfully aware of this and Winston's position in the Ministry of Truth gave him even greater opportunity to experience the unmaking and remaking of history: 'All history was a palimpsest,' he said, 'scraped clean and reinscribed as often as was necessary.' In *The Book of Laughter and Forgetting*,[42] Kundera, after giving an example of the kind of work in which Winston himself was involved – the airbrushing out from old photographs of discredited influential figures – declares that the individual is as much a rewriter of history as the party. 'People are always shouting they want to create a better future. It's not true . . . The only reason people want to be masters of the future is to change the past.' It is our past that gives us weight and substance, that provides the shape to our self-conceit. Kundera's character sums Orwell's argument up succinctly: 'The struggle of man against power is the struggle of memory against forgetting.' In Oceania the state controls the past and the individual has no memory. Winston Smith is the last individual in Oceania.

Another prerequisite for full individuality, according to Orwell, is family life.[43] In Oceania family life among Party members has broken down entirely. Inner Party members, it will be remembered, have no family. As for the Outer Party, 'the family had become in effect an extension of the Thought Police. It was a device by means of which everyone could be surrounded night and day by informers who knew him intimately.' The model of Oceanian family life is provided by Winston's near neighbours in Victory Mansions, the Parsons. Parsons himself, than whom a more stalwart and hearty Party member could not be imagined, was eventually betrayed to the Thought Police by his own daughter. But Parsons' predicament was far from unique. 'It was almost normal for people over thirty to be frightened of their children.' The Party had destroyed love and family loyalties and thus deprived the individual of the sustenance that these provide. One of Winston's most enduring memories was of his mother, dying without reproach so that he might live. This act belonged to a former time 'when there was still privacy, love and friendship, and when the members of a family stood by one another without needing to know the reason'. As a focus for loyalty and love and a bastion of privacy the family was a role that the totalitarian state had needed to smash.

Indeed, when reviewing a book on radical rehousing programmes in 1946 Orwell noted that the planners sought as a priority to preserve family life: 'a deep instinct warns them not to destroy the family, which in the modern world is the sole refuge from the state'.[44]

Next Orwell claimed participation in a cultural background for the individual, who needed to feel part of a tradition which represented his or her beliefs and aspirations and which he or she could hope to pass on to their children. For Orwell the most important part of that tradition was language. It is arguably the case that he attached more importance to the nature and function of language than most political theorists and philosophers.

In Oceania the task of the party philologists, like Syme (a man too creative to survive for long), was systematically to control and restrict vocabulary in the belief that behaviour would thus also be controllable. The linguistic analysts believed that behaviour and indeed consciousness were causally related to the nature and structure of language. Syme's claim is no less ambitious: the more vocabulary contracts, the more the Party will be able to control behaviour. 'Don't you see,' he explains to Winston, 'that the whole aim of Newspeak is to narrow the range of thought? In the end we shall make thoughtcrime literally impossible because there will be no words in which to express it.'[45] In an appendix, 'The Principles of Newspeak', Orwell provides an example of Syme's work. The Newspeak word 'sexcrime' covered all sexual misdemeanours such as fornication, adultery, homosexual acts and other 'perversions'. But it also covered 'normal-intercourse practised for its own sake. Before long then, intercourse for its own sake would come to be seen as just as reprehensible as, say, raping a minor. Moreover, Newspeak encompasses all moral judgements within composites based upon the unit word 'good'. Thus: good, ungood, doublegood, doubleplusungood and so on, thereby rendering the making of all but the crudest moral distinctions impossible. If this were not enough, the system of thought known as 'Doublethink' by which two contradictory opinions may be held simultaneously makes it impossible for any individual to perceive, let alone articulate or communicate, the truth. The political importance of language as a repository of cultural pride has long been appreciated. Thus in Victorian times the British government tried to eradicate the use of the Welsh and Scottish and Irish languages in a quest for cultural and political homogeneity. When, as a consequence of pressure and a more enlightened attitude, cultural diversity became accepted, the policy was reversed.

Kundera, by contrast, does not accept the primacy of language in protecting or destroying a culture.[46]

> 'The first step in liquidating a people,' said Hubl, 'is to erase its memory. Destroy its books, its culture, its history. Then have someone write new books, manufacture a new culture, invent a new history. Before long the nation will begin to forget what it is and what it was . . .'
>
> 'What about language?'
>
> 'Why would anyone bother to take it from us? It will soon be a matter of folklore and die a natural death.'

In *Nineteen Eighty-four* Winston attempts to re-establish connections with a vanished culture so as to erect a barrier against the Party. The book he bought as a diary was an elegant, old one with smooth, creamy paper. He bought it in Charrington's junk shop, to which he had been instinctively drawn. Then he bought himself a paperweight, a beautiful piece of crystal but without any use. 'If [the lifestyle of the past] survives anywhere, it's in a few solid objects, with no words attached to them, like that lump of glass there,' Winston remarks. The room above the junk shop which Winston and his lover Julia rented from Charrington is described as 'a world, a pocket of the past where extinct animals could walk'. In such a world Winston became whole again, his nagging leg-ulcer briefly cured. Predictably enough, when the Thought Police finally broke into the room one of them smashed the paperweight on the hearthstone, symbolically breaking all connections with the values of the previous culture, and indeed shattering the 'crystal spirit' which epitomised those values (and which, in Spain, Orwell had believed unbreakable). Winston's claim to a cultural heritage was also exemplified by his toast in O'Brien's flat, when he mistakenly believed that he was being recruited into the Brotherhood: 'To the Past!' His first diary entry, a dedication, had also been 'to the future, or to the past, to a time when thought is free, when men are different from one another and do not live alone — to a time when truth exists and what is done cannot be undone.' It is the memory of this now-dead culture which calls to Winston through the half-remembered nursery rhyme 'Oranges and Lemons'. Charrington is able to complete the rhyme: the Party recognises and understands its enemies.

Franz Kafka's was a world whose umbilical cord to the values of a past culture had been broken, a world whose humanity 'has lost all continuity with humanity, a humanity that no longer knows anything, that lives in nameless cities with nameless streets or streets with names different from the ones they had yesterday, because a name means continuity with the past and people without a past are people without a name'.[47] Kafka's was a world of totalitarian nightmare.

Orwell's next claim for the individual was for a full emotional life. He believed that a totalitarian élite would, sooner or later, seek to control human emotions: indeed, as we know, in Oceania the Party was already at work on abolishing the orgasm. All feelings of passion would henceforth be directed towards the Party and used by the Party. The love of Big Brother represents its positive manifestation, hatred directed either to the external threat of Eastasia or Eurasia; the internal threat of Goldstein and the Brotherhood represents the negative. Julie's great attraction for Winston was her vaunted promiscuity, her simple love of carnal pleasures. When they were first alone in the hazel grove, Winston described Julia's quickly unzipping her clothing and flinging it aside as a gesture which seemed to be annihilating a whole civilisation. He was fully aware of, indeed rejoiced in, the treasonable nature of sexual pleasure. 'Listen,' he says to Julia, 'The more men you've had, the more I love you . . . I hate purity, I hate goodness! I don't want any virtue to exist anywhere. I want everybody to be corrupt to the bone.'[48] Promiscuity, Winston recognised, would provide 'a force that would tear the Party to pieces'. It is doubtful if Orwell believed that widespread promiscuity was a necessary political virtue, that it would provide a sound basis for a liberal democracy for example. It has to be remembered that he supported promiscuity in much the same way as he supported assassination and other acts of terrorism − as demanded by the times. This is not meant to be a eulogising of sexual licence for its own sake. Indeed, Smith later accuses Julia scornfully of being 'only a rebel from the waist down'. Irving Howe argues that eroticism and not love is the enemy of the state in *Nineteen Eighty-four*. He is only partly right:[49] in room 101 it is love which is cleansed from Winston.

Orwell also claims material sufficiency as a precondition for a full life for the individual. Winston has some ancestral memory which causes him to reject as unnatural the discomfort, the dirt and the scarcity, of life in Oceania. Man has a right to something better than Victory Mansions with its 'lifts that never work, the cold water, the cigarettes that came to pieces, the food with its strange, evil tastes'; a right to something better than a world in which 'nearly everyone was ugly, and would have been ugly even if dressed otherwise than in the uniform blue overalls'. It was deliberate party policy to maintain a condition of scarcity for all but members of the Inner Party so as to enhance the importance of even minor privileges. The struggle for day-to-day necessities, says Orwell, wears down the human spirit and denies individuality.

Lastly Orwell argues for the importance of individual privacy, for the existence of a private world into which a person could securely retire. It was the *privateness* of the British way of life which Orwell cherished. A home of your own to do what you like in. That was why 'the most hateful of all names in an English ear is Nosey Parker'.[50] But Oceania's telescreens make privacy impossible and because Big Brother might be watching, people are obliged to walk about with an expression of quiet optimism; the portrayal of any other emotion could be construed as treason. The temple of privacy is, as we have seen, inside the skull, and Orwell wanted to make it plain that the temple was no longer sacrosanct. The human being, he wrote in 1944, is not autonomous. Defoe could never actually have written *Robinson Crusoe* on a desert island, nor could any philosopher, scientist or artist exist in isolation; 'they need constant stimulation from other people, it is about impossible to think without talking'. So: by taking away freedom of speech and by weakening the desire for intellectual freedom through socialisation, the space inside the skull becomes not a temple of privacy and liberty but a void.[51] Simply stated, this need for privacy is nothing less than a *sine qua non* for a full life for the individual.

The right and capacity to form one's own judgement on external events; a rich and sustaining family life, cultural continuity, based upon a vibrant language, a full emotional life, a life of reasonable material sufficiency and finally a completely private world into which one could retire: these were the bastions of identity which Winston Smith sought to defend. The obliteration of the private realm, the elimination of personal and cultural identity so that nothing stood between the atomised individual and the state: this was the programme of the Party.

Winston's revolt ends in total defeat. On the final page of the novel we find him remade, whole and unalienated for the first time in his adult life, reflecting on his futile struggle:

O cruel, needless misunderstanding! O stubborn, self-willed exile from the loving breast! Two gin-scented tears trickled down the side of his nose. But it was alright, the struggle was finished. He had won a victory over himself. He loved Big Brother.

Nineteen Eighty-four has had a considerable influence on post-war political thinking. With the collapse of the Soviet Union its influence should remain just as strong, for it stands as a warning of what a modern technological world might be like without the political values which Orwell cherished. It stands as a warning as to which values must be defended if a reasonable life is to remain available to the individual in the next millennium. It stands as a warning to socialists and progressives (and indeed to radical conservatives) that leaders must never be allowed to lose touch with the values of the rank-and-file. It provides a yardstick with which we can measure the extent to which our atomised, technological, mass-communications-based, observer (perhaps voyeur) society is heading for the world of Big Brother and the Party. If Nineteen Eighty-four seems an exaggerated impossibility, Small reminds us[52] that the Nazi's final solution to the 'Jewish problem' had already been parodied over two hundred and fifty years before, by Swift's Houyhnhnms debating the final solution of the Yahoo problem – to expel them from the 'arse-hole of the world'. As Patrick Reilly succinctly asks: 'Who writes a warning against an impossibility?'[53]

6 Orwellian socialism today

'What is decency?'
'Something your kind will never understand.
We have replaced decency by reason.' (Arthur Koestler, *Darkness at Noon*)

Few writers on politics have left behind a more ambiguous legacy than
George Orwell. When one considers how relatively short his writing
career was and how little he actually wrote, this is suprising. It is not
appropriate here to consider the arguments by which Orwell has been
claimed for anarchism,[1] Trotskyism,[2] democratic socialism,[3] English
patriotism,[4] tory traditionalism[5] and even protestant individualism;[6]
none of these claims can be dismissed entirely, though none of them
comes near to providing a full description of what, for want of a better
word, might be called 'Orwellism'.

Perhaps we can get nearer to a full description by considering two
lines of criticism of Orwellism which are fairly common. The first and
more sophisticated argues that Orwellism was never more than a
rather vague moralistic hankering after equality which lacked intellectual coherence and analytical depth. The second argues that Orwell
abandoned the early optimistic socialism of *Road to Wigan Pier* and
Homage to Catalonia for the basically pessimistic and anti-socialist individualism of *Animal Farm* and *Nineteen Eighty-four*. According to these
arguments Orwell was shallow or inconsistent and possibly both. No
wonder his legacy is ambiguous.

The criticism that Orwell's political writing was shallow is clearly a
damning one. Raymond Williams claimed that while criticising its
excesses Orwell simply did not understand the nature of capitalism as
an economic and political system.[7] David Kubal argued that Orwell's
'inability or unwillingness to ask philosophical questions narrows the
value of his political thought'.[8] More comprehensively, Trilling suggested that Orwell's virtue as a political writer resided precisely in this
shallowness. He was not a profound thinker but one who confronted

the world with 'nothing else than one's simple, direct, undeceived intelligence'.[9]

Well, it is true that Orwell forsook ideology. But it is not true that he was ignorant about it. Richard Rees recalls a debate at an *Adelphi* summer school in 1936 between Orwell, who was lecturing on the conditions of the poor, and some Marxists. 'Without any parade of learning he produced breath-taking Marxist paradoxes and epigrams in such a way as to make the sacred mysteries seem almost too obvious and simple.'[10] We know from his reviews that Orwell was widely read, in political philosophy and history as well as literature (French as well as English). He *chose* to forsake ideology, claiming that he felt uneasy getting away from the 'ordinary world where grass is green, stones are hard, etc.'.[11] In his defence of Shakespeare against Tolstoy's celebrated onslaught, Orwell remarked admiringly that, like most Englishmen, Skakespeare had no philosophical facility, only a code of conduct. In fact Orwell forsook ideology in rather the same way as a mystic could be said to forsake theology. Like the mystic, Orwell was more interested in developing a moral code which, again like the mystic, he believed was not capable of being properly articulated in the traditional intellectual manner. The Christian mystics attempted to follow the moral code expounded by Christ, and it is abundantly clear that Christ himself sought to express the basic precepts of this moral code not through doctrinal or theological exegesis but through simple parables drawn from everyday life. What Christ sought to provide were concrete examples of a moral code in action. As Dietrich Bonhoeffer said, Christ 'leads us away from any kind of abstract ethic and towards an ethic which is entirely concrete'.[12] It would be nothing less than absurd to suggest that Christianity was limited as a consequence of this approach; indeed its concreteness has been its strength for two thousand years. There is no reason to suppose that a political morality might not similarly be stronger for having abjured ideology.

But a moral code needs roots and if it is not rooted in an ideology, what does provide its sustenance? To answer this question as far as Orwellism is concerned we must turn back to his attitude towards Christianity. I have suggested that he had an ambiguous stance *vis-à-vis* the Church and the faith. On the one hand it is likely that his account of Dorothy's loss of faith in *A Clergyman's Daughter* was autobiographical, and yet on the other that loss of faith is itself indecisive. Not only does Dorothy recognise the importance of faith but she decides to continue to live as if she still believed. Reference has been made to the two occasions on which Orwell used the analogy of a wasp eating jam from his plate. Orwell cut him in half but the wasp paid no attention, continuing to eat while the jam trickled out of his oesophagus. Only as it tried to fly away did the wasp fully appreciate what had become of it. 'It is the same with modern man. The thing that has been cut away is his soul . . . .'[13] Modern man, in forsaking belief in the afterlife, had lost his soul, his *raison d'être*. A believer can accommodate himself to the fact that man who is born of woman has but a short time to live and is full of misery, because it is not this life but life in eternity that counts. But as Orwell says, it is quite another thing 'to admit that life is full of misery when you believe that the grave really finishes you'.[14] Life without the soul is a life without value and there are only three possible ways, according to Orwell, of dealing with that. The first is to retreat to religion, the second to work unendingly and the third to lose oneself in what he called sluttish antinomianism. Dorothy, and perhaps Orwell, chose a mixture of the first two and rejected the third.

I have argued that Orwell was very defensive about his religious affiliations in the 1930s, but it is clear that the practices of the Church of England remained important to him. Both his marriage and his funeral services were conducted according to the rites of the Church of England. That fact cannot be dismissed as an eccentricity, still less an irrelevance. His specific antipathy to the Roman Catholic Church can be understood much better as a measure of Anglican commitment than of atheism. If a level of residual commitment remained, why keep quiet about it? I have suggested that he probably considered it politically expedient not to make anything of it – it would have limited his room for manoeuvre – and that he did not wish to be associated with any 'ism'. In his own words: 'I should say that it is a good rule of thumb never to mention religion if you can possibly avoid it.'[15].

A number of those who knew Orwell acknowledged his residual Christianity. W. H. Auden wrote: 'If I were asked to name people I considered true Christians, the name of George Orwell is one of the first that would come to mind.'[16] Spender put the same point rather differently, projecting Orwell's attitude to life as Christ-like. He called Orwell 'an innocent, a kind of English Candide of the twentieth century. He believes that 2 + 2 = 4; and that what happens, happens. The consequences of really believing this are shattering. Christ was brought up as a carpenter in a carpenter's shop.'[17] Christopher Hollis argued that Orwell never doubted for a moment that man was fundamentally a moral being and that this world was a testing place.[18] Finally, and more broadly, Connolly said that Orwell could not use a handkerchief without moralising on conditions in the handkerchief industry. Let us be clear: Orwell was no card-carrying Anglican. He explicitly wrote that his moral code was not to be considered exclusively Christian, for that would weaken it.[19] He would no doubt have found a place for any religion which enhanced and did not diminish the individual. Moreover, just as he saw some socialists as the chief objection to socialism, so he saw some Christians as the chief objection to Christianity.[20] Nevertheless his moral system was much more essentially Judaeo-Christian than he saw fit to admit. George Orwell may have been an atheist; Eric Blair was no such thing.

In conceding man's spiritual nature, Orwell was aware of the irony of man's recent liberation from superstition. By refuting the myths of established religion, man had left himself peculiarly vulnerable. He had sawn away the branch on which he was seated. 'But unfortunately there had been a little mistake. The thing at the bottom was not a bed of roses but a cesspool full of barbed wire.' What was to be done? As he saw it the problem was 'to restore the religious attitude while accepting death as final'.[21] The answer was to restore man's faith in innate decency. I have already alluded to the fact that what he wrote about Dickens could easily be applied to Orwell himself. He wrote that Dickens was a believer though formal religion played little part in his life. 'Where he is a Christian is in his quasi-instinctive siding with the oppressed against the oppressors.' When he attacked the practices of various Victorian institutions, it was not so much the institutions themselves that Dickens was against as what Chesterton called 'an expression on a human face'. That expression was oppression; the face of the powerful. What Dickens championed was the 'native decency of the common man'; as Orwell says, he was 'the standard bearer of common decency'. As we have already noted, after attacking Dickens's 'utter lack of any constructive suggestion anywhere in his work', and his enormous platitude that 'if men would behave decently the world would be decent', Orwell came to the view that there was much in what Dickens had to say. He came to see that the decency of a moral code in which good and evil could be identified was more important than particular kinds of economic, social and political systems. The vast majority of ordinary people, he argued (like Dickens), believe in common decency, without the need to 'tie it up with any transcendental belief'.[22] In other words, they believe in a system of good and evil independent of heaven and hell.[23] In defending Dickens, Orwell was, in a sense, replying to the attacks later made upon himself by Raymond Williams, Samuel Hynes and others.

In locating his morality among the powerless, Orwell was following Dickens, but he was prepared to go further and to be more analytical. His premise is that the traditional Judaeo-Christian moral values could be equated with decency. They had not died but lived on in the lives of ordinary working-people in working-class communities. In an article on Charlie Chaplin, he suggests that the comedian's success was based upon his ability to symbolise 'the ineradicable belief in decency that exists in the hearts of ordinary people . . . Everywhere, under the surface, the common man sticks obstinately to the belief that he derives from the Christian culture.'[24]

Orwell explored this congruity of values in some depth in his essay *The Art of Donald McGill*;[25] it was crucial to his thinking. The world which McGill depicts has much appeal for Orwell.[26] It is the world of the oppressed and it represents a worm's eye view. It is a world in which those with incomes much above or below £5 a week are figures of fun. It is a world of superficial obscenity, well presented by McGill's postcards, but not of pornography – rather, a skit on pornography. They possess a meaning, he claims, only in relation to a fairly strict moral code, the backbone of which is a strong belief in marriage and family life. It is a world in which family loyalties are put first, a world 'more traditional, more in accord with the Christian past than [that of] the well-to-do women who still try to look young at forty'. All the obscenities, the *double-entendres* of McGill's world imply a common culture strong enough not to see these as threats. They reflect a world in which people 'want to be good, but not too good, and not quite all the time'.

This culture is staunchly patriotic, yet it goes in for a mild guying of patriotism. Orwell writes that he cannot hear proclamations by Great Men, major speeches by Fuhrers, pious moral proclamations by left-wing parties, Papal pronouncements and the like, without also 'seeming to hear in the background a chorus of raspberries from all the millions of common men'. For Orwell, Donald McGill and his colleagues reflect the 'ancient wisdom' which makes the working class the most reliable enemy of totalitarianism .

In a review of a novel by a working class author, Orwell wrote:

> All the time that one reads one seems to . . . hear the voice of innumerable industrial workers whom [the author] typifies. These are the voices of a normally silent multitude. All over England, in every industrial town, there are men by scores of thousands whose attitude to life, if only they could express it . . . would change the whole consciousness of our race.[27]

In another review, this time of a novel by his friend Jack Common, he wrote championing the authentic voice of the ordinary man, whose circumstances positively encourage loyalty, generosity and a hatred of privilege. If such people could only have a say in major events their influence would be transformative. In practice, however, they tend to get no further than 'the trenches, the sweatshop and the jail'. As a consequence, he concluded, one is almost 'driven to the cynical thought that men are only decent when they are powerless'.[28]

If it is accepted that Orwell sought to articulate a moral system based upon Christian values, what right had he to call it socialism? Samuel Hynes wrote that Orwell's commitment was not strictly socialist at all but what he called an emotional liberalism which said nothing more than 'if men would be decent the world would be decent'.[29] In fact this is a superficial judgement. The moral system which Orwell sought to propagate belonged, or so he believed, to a class, and to one class only, the working class (and those on its fringes). Moreover, in order for this moral system to become generally established it would be necessary, as Orwell argued unequivocally in *The Road To Wigan Pier*, for the middle class to sink its prejudices and choose to become working class. Behaving decently had sociological references. What is more, Orwell made it quite clear that his moral system required equality as a *sine qua non*. Decency, then, was a more precise idea than the phrase emotional liberalism allows. Moreover, Orwell believed that for his decency – socialism – to succeed, it would have to grow naturally out of the dispositions of ordinary people – the only hope for it, in other words, lay with the proles – and it had most to fear from the middle-class intellectuals who claimed to believe in it and who sought to transform it into an ideological system which ordinary people would not even understand.

I would like now to deal briefly with Trilling's observation that Orwell's reputation resided in his simple, undeceived intelligence. We have already observed that the 'Orwell' of the undeceived intelligence is a character created by Eric Blair through whom the author's own political views, dressed up as if they were really the readers', percolate: 'Orwell' is the personification of the undeceived intelligence. When he sees, he sees with our eyes; when he thinks it is our thoughts he articulates. This constitutes a considerable literary feat and, more significantly, the proselytist's undetected sleight of hand. Far from being the happy coincidence Trilling seems to suggest, we have observed how this character was painstakingly chiselled out of the experiences of Orwell's apprenticeship, the achievement of years of failure and hardship. Orwell's so-called superficiality was a matter of conscious choice. To put it bluntly, he thought there were more important aspects to socialism than ideology.

I want now to explore the second line of criticism – that of inconsistency. It is not my intention to claim that his work was toweringly consistent throughout. It is not difficult to find striking inconsistencies between and within his works (indeed an important inconsistency in his assessment of Dickens has already been alluded to). What I have in mind rather, is to challenge the view that the main thrust of his politics underwent a major change. To claim that Orwell is more consistent than is usually granted is to argue that the major political statements to be found in his earlier work contain essentially the same message as those found in his later works. This claim can be tested easily enough by comparing what has been said about Orwell's earlier and later works.

Prior to writing *Wigan Pier*, Orwell showed himself to be obsessed with guilt at being one of the oppressors in the imperialist system in Burma. When he returned to England he simply transposed the imperial theme of oppressors and oppressed into the domestic industrial setting, classifying the owning class as the oppressors and the working class as the oppressed. Perhaps he became only gradually aware that it was the values of the oppressed which offered the basis of the good life; perhaps he had always wanted to believe something like this. In any case, by the time he came to write *Wigan Pier*, he had a pretty clear idea about where the good life was to be found: not among the lumpenproletariat of Paris and London, not among the aimless and dispirited like the Brookers (who were primarily responsible for the sordid conditions in which they chose to live), not among the sheep of Animal Farm who could only bleat to instructions; no, the good life was to be found with the better-off, more stable section of the working class.

The most immediate and indeed the most durable impression which the North of England made upon Orwell, it will be remembered, was one of equality. This sense of equality, he says, is deeply rooted in family life and characteristic of social relations among the working class in general. There can be no doubt that he responded to the warmth of working-class family life throughout his career, continually drawing nourishment from it in his prose style as well as his politics: 'In a [comparatively prosperous] working-class home you can breathe a warm, decent, deeply human atmosphere which is not so easy to find elsewhere.'[30] In such a sane and comely home working people are more likely to be happy than the better-off and better-educated. Socialism for Orwell was the living out, at the public level, of these private values and so, by definition, Orwell's working man represented the clearest expression of basic socialist values.

The arguments set out in chapter 3 may be summarised as follows: working-class socialism is non-ideological, non-utopian, non-progressive, non- (maybe even anti-) intellectual. It cannot be elaborated into a programme for action because it represents not so much a set of policies as a caste of mind. This caste of mind is not shared by socialist ideologues who tend to be motivated by a hatred of squalor and poverty. Poverty is something to be abolished from above, if necessary, by violence. Orwell believed that this disgust of poverty, expressed for example in the so-called gospel according to St Andrew Undershaft in Shaw's *Major Barbara*, really masked a hatred of the poor which found its natural shape in totalitarian rule. Moreover, since to abolish poverty from above would *ipso facto* destroy Orwell's socialist values, he regarded it as throwing out the baby with the bathwater.

The task Orwell set himself, consequently, was to rid socialism of the kind of ideological straitjacket imposed by these writers, to portray socialism not as intellectualised but humanised, with a commitment above all to justice and liberty, which was what socialism meant when all the nonsense was stripped off. What socialism needed was a propagandist who could speak out for its primal sanities; 'less about "class consciousness", "expropriation of the expropriators", "bourgeois ideology" and "proletarian solidarity" . . . and more about justice, liberty, and the plight of the unemployed'. Thus, almost from the beginning of his writing career, Orwell had not only chosen a role for himself from which he never departed but he had established a brand of socialism rooted in the working-class values of solidarity, equality and what he called decency and justice. To suggest that until these values were articulated in a coherent ideology they were as good as meaningless was to miss the point entirely. Ordinary people *already knew* what they meant; they already operated successfully in working-class life at both the private and the public level. It was in this sense that Orwell's socialism was concrete: a way of living one's life rather than a blueprint for restructuring society. Orwell was to remain the champion of working-class socialism all his life, was to remain the enemy of socialist ideologues, was to mistrust material 'progress' and technological development because they threatened the working-class way of life.

Homage to Catalonia indicates that Orwell's Spanish experiences only strengthened his faith in working-class values, only reaffirmed in his mind the connection between these values and the underlying ideals of socialism and – a new development – brought him briefly to see the working class in Marxist terms, as a potentially revolutionary force.

If Spain heightened Orwell's perception of what socialism was it also strengthened his convictions about what it was not. He came to believe, and with good reason, that the Republic (and the revolution) had been betrayed by the ideologists and intellectuals: betrayed by the 'Marxist' ideologists in Moscow and thus by Spain's communist ideologists, betrayed by left-wing intellectuals in Britain who had sought to hide the fact that the communists in Spain were imprisoning and killing their anarchist and Trotskyist allies, and thus also killing the idea that republican Spain was revolutionary. Moreover Orwell saw intellectuals conniving at the creation of newspaper reports which, he claimed, bore no relation whatever to the truth. This deliberate falsification of observable, 'objective' truth came to dominate Orwell's later thinking but represents an extension of, not a departure from, 'Orwellism'.

Orwell's next major political work, *Animal Farm*, was a story of revolution betrayed. From the beginning Orwell makes it clear which of the animals are to be considered virtuous. Chief amongst these are the horses Boxer and Clover. They possess the qualities of warmth and compassion which mark out Orwell's proletarians. Yet the horses' political capacities did not match up to their compassion. They were unaware of the extent to which the pigs had begun to dominate all aspects of life on the farm and to subvert animalism. The fate of Boxer provides the book's bitterest irony. He was the backbone of Napoleon's workforce, his by far the greatest contribution to the building of the windmill which was the linchpin of Napoleon's programme of electrification. When the windmill was destroyed Boxer rebuilt it virtually alone, working on through pain and disappointment into sickness until eventually he collapsed. Nobody could forget how Napoleon repaid his loyalty, and the nature of his subsequent demise indicated that the revolutionary potential of the working class, so clearly symbolised in Boxer, could be bled dry in a revolution dominated by intellectuals, as left-wing revolutions so far have tended to be.

The pigs, of course, are the villains of the story; not only Napoleon but all the pigs, even the banished Trotsky-figure Snowball. Their relationship with the other animals is meant to stand exactly for the relationship between the intellectuals and the proletariat in any socialist revolution: the intellectuals would dominate and their interest was power and all its trappings, no more and no less. Moreover, Orwell's Spanish experiences and knowledge of events in Russia led him to believe that the intellectuals would, like Napoleon, use that power mercilessly. The cart-horses, by way of complete contrast, possess the warmth and compassion that mark out Orwell's working class. When Major first made his speech outlining the principles of animalism, the smaller animals squeezed in near the two horses for comfort and protection, as if the objectives of animalism were being sanctioned by the warmth and support of the horses. Later in the story, after one of the post-revolutionary show trials, when it finally dawns on the animals collectively that the revolution has failed them, they again turn to Clover for comfort, huddling around her, not speaking. Clover's deep sense of melancholy is communicated to the other animals; she realises too late that decency, justice, compassion, 'humanity', have been subverted. So both at the beginning and at the end of the revolution it is the values of the horses – proletarian values – which measure its success.

Once more Orwell kept to his major themes. *Animal Farm* illustrates the resilience and compassion of ordinary 'people' and by contrast the harsh face of ideology. He had come to believe that the intellectuals he had never trusted were capable of making socialism into a political system every bit as totalitarian and terrifying as a fascist state.

Talk of totalitarianism leads inevitably to *Nineteen Eighty-four*. I argued earlier that in most respects the book continues with the themes established in *Animal Farm*, a state established by a socialist revolution and run by intellectuals through a spurious ideology known as Ingsoc

(English socialism). The working class stands outside the polity to all intents and purposes, its own value system intact, facing inwards, concentrating upon its own survival, and not outwards, upon the conquest of power.

Winston's attitude to the proles changes during the novel, symbolising Orwell's own retreat from his belief in the revolutionary potential of the working class. At the beginning he rather despises the proles, noting that their lives are full of quarrels with neighbours, football, beer, gambling and so on. His own attempts to make contact with them are disastrous yet Winston retains the idea that if there was any hope it was with the proles, an idea which is true doublethink, embodying both mystical truth and palpable absurdity.[31] Reminding us briefly of Boxer, Winston declares:

> They need only to rise up and shake themselves like a horse shaking off flies. If they chose they could blow the party to pieces tomorrow morning. Surely sooner or later it must occur to them to do it? And yet . . . .

Winston comes to recognise that his belief in the revolutionary potential of the proles has no base and we can assume that O'Brien's insistence during the interrogation that the proles would never revolt, not in a thousand years, not in a million, thoroughly convinces him. But in one crucial sense this no longer signified, for he has come to realise that hope lies with the proles only because their values would survive, and for no other reason. Winston recognised that their instinctive loyalty was not to any system but to each other and that there was a moral force, and indeed a political value, in their very gestures of love, compassion and understanding: in their code of decency. He no longer despised them or thought of the proles 'as an inert force which would one day spring to life and regenerate the world'. The proles, he came to realise, had stayed human. They had not become hardened inside. They had retained their instinctive values of decency and common compassion.

Although the proles are on the fringe both of Oceanian society and of the action, it is their values which provide the only warmth in the novel. For example, when Winston is with Julia in their room above the antique shop his attention is drawn to singing from outside. It was a prole woman 'solid as a Norman pillar, with brawny red arms' hanging nappies on a line. She was singing a song devised by a mechanical versificator but she sang with such feeling as to tranform the 'deadful rubbish' into an expression of human feeling. Later in the book Winston's attention was drawn to a similar sight and sound, a prole woman with thick arms, 'powerful, mare-like buttocks' and 'a solid, contourless body like a block of granite'. She had endured a life of endless domestic chores, first for her children and then for her grandchildren. And at the end, indomitable, she was still singing. There are other examples of proletarian values poking through the surface of this bleak narrative. When Winston visits a cinema and sees a newsflash of an Oceanian helicopter dropping a bomb on a lifeboat full of enemy women and children, a woman down in the prole part of the cinema starts to kick up a fuss. She shouts, 'they didn't oughter of showed it not in front of the kids they didn't it ain't right not in front of the kids it ain't'. She was turned out, though nothing would happen to her – nobody cares what the proles say. Later, Winston's life was saved by the prompt action of a prole during an air-raid. The very survival of these values was a political triumph, for their continued existence was always a potential threat to the Party.

The theme of proletarian values dominates *Nineteen Eighty-four* by its very absence, and is precisely the theme which dominates all Orwell's work. From 1936 Orwell tried to characterise socialism as a moral system based upon the values of the stable working class. After a brief flirtation with the Marxist notion of a successful class war, Orwell concluded that revolutions did not provide the kind of medium in which his socialism could grow. This left the possibility that it would grow slowly as more and more of the 'oppressed' recognised the moral worth and sheer common sense and moral superiority of socialism. Orwell's chief originality lies in his unequivocal assertion in *Wigan Pier* that the slow process would be greatly accelerated if the middle classes, himself included, gave up their social aspirations and sank 'without further struggles into the working class where we belong'. Orwell's own contribution was more positive; he made himself the mouthpiece of working-class socialism not by elevating it into a coherent ideology but by concretising it in his literature so skilfully that it would be perverse to claim not to have understood what he meant. What is more, he attempted, with some success, to live his own life according to the socialist principles he associated with the working class.

All this is not to say that we need to agree with him. Having defended Orwell against the allegations of superficiality and inconsistency, I would like briefly to suggest three lines of criticism of Orwell's working-class socialism which are possibly more sustainable.

The first suggests that Orwell's working class simply does not possess the virtues which he attributed to it, or perhaps that if the values once existed, they no longer do. The second is that even if such values existed or indeed still exist, they form a basis for social living and not for political action and, after all, even Machiavelli recognised the civic importance of private virtue, though of course it had no part in his statecraft. My third criticism is that, even accepting the existence of these Orwellian virtues for the sake of argument, they represent the reflexes of the working class to its general conditions of servitude and material insufficiency. Remove these exigent pressures and the virtues become redundant and wither away.

It is certainly true that a major characteristic of British working-class life, especially in the North of England, has traditionally been its manifest inequality – between the sexes. Orwell has very little indeed to say about this, referring only briefly (and without comment) to the fact that unemployed men generally did nothing to help around the house, refusing to be 'Sally Annes'. He also chooses to ignore the considerable amount of evidence of tyrannical father-son relationships as exemplified in the work of D. H. Lawrence, himself the son of a miner. Moreover he has nothing to say about the violence which is and always was a feature of working-class life in major British cities (read accounts of major soccer games before the First World War for example, especially between rivals, such as Glagow Rangers and Celtic; read of working-class communities torn apart by bitter industrial disputes such as London's docklands in 1911). If we now take the second line of criticism, that Orwell's values pertain to the private and not the public realm, we might reasonably have expected Orwell to have offered evidence from the trade union movement or even the Labour party to indicate that working-class political institutions, which the unions certainly were and the Labour party arguably was at this time, operated rather differently to bourgeois institutions. He chose not to do so and we are therefore free to conclude if we wish that this was because they were no different and that working-class values simply did not survive the hot-house of politics. Nowadays it could be argued that the characteristic 'gentleness' of the British has given way to the mindless hooliganism of the lager louts, to a police force frequently armed and subject to an ever-increasing number of citizens' complaints, to bus drivers refusing to drive to certain working-class areas in some cities after dark for fear of violence, and to a bellicose, jingoistic people's press which is an affront to every value Orwell prized.

Finally, the argument that working-class values are the natural de-fence mechanism of a community under pressure. Illidge, a working-class character in Huxley's *Point Counter Point*, made the telling obser-vation that, living on less than £4 per week, you 'damned well got to behave like a Christian'. You needed the support of your neighbours to deal with life's problems. However, the working class has become more affluent since Orwell's day, and the need for the support of an active local community has declined. The direct accretion of greater wealth has had its effect, as has the welfare state through its health, income support, education and housing policies; both these have ten-ded to erode working-class communities in a comprehensive manner. The almost tribal social framework into which working-class children were generally born until the 1960s has not disappeared but it is by no means as widespread. It can be questioned whether traditional working-class values have survived the transformation from the typical close-knit back-to-back communities to the high-rise estates. While it is true that these developments occurred after Orwell's death it is nonetheless also true that he did not address the possibility that the values he admired, a consequence of poverty, would not survive better targeted state welfare. He opposed 'progress' for fear of its effect on working-class communities, but he did not oppose welfare.

And finally, what are we to make of Orwell's criticism of intellec-tuals? Two interpretations of his fiercely critical picture of them have been suggested: the first that he seemed to think that intellectuals were actual or potential sadists; the second, and more persuasive, that power corrupted all people. If there is anything in the first, then we can see why Orwell directed much of his criticism towards British socialist intellectuals, for it was they who sought to concentrate power in the hands of the state, they who dominated the socialist movement – after all, was not the Conservative party 'the stupid party'? Since Orwell's death the Labour party in Britain has lost much of its tradi-tional working-class activism. Many traditionally strong industrial constituencies have come under the control of young middle-class intellectuals. These people would argue that the party has become more socialist as a consequence but then, that would not make the party safe against totalitarian tendencies in Orwell's eyes; in fact quite the reverse. Yet Orwell's critics would feel cheated unless he could explain to them how a party could expect to operate without firm leadership; and again, there is no clear answer in his writings. Rodden goes so far as to suggest that Orwell's politics were marked more by a rancour against the intelligentsia than any positive identification with the working class. It was this that ' shaped his self-image and reputation as an intellectual's working-man'.[32] Rodden goes too far. A paraphrase of Orwell's own attitude towards revolutionary Barcelona is probably as good an indication of his general attitude towards the working class as we will get: there was much about them that he did not understand, some things he did not even like; but he knew that their values were worth fighting for.

Despite these potentially damning criticisms, Conor Cruise O'Brien concluded admiringly that Orwell's effect on the British left, like Voltaire's on the French nobility, was commendably salutary: 'he weakened their belief in their own ideology, made them ashamed of their clichés, left them intellectually more scrupulous and defenceless'.[33] If he managed this, it was a great achievement. Richard Rees compared Orwell to Simone Weil, in that both understood the balance of society and added their weight to the lighter scale. Orwell took his stance 'like justice, that fugitive from the victor's camp'. Yet the stakes in Orwell's game were different. He sought to strip the superstructure of ideology from contemporary socialism, revealing it at base to be a concrete moral system concerned with common humanity which, despite its many defects, he genuinely believed to be the best hope for mankind.

But was he wrong? Was his working class a chimera? I have endeavoured to show that he painted a fairly sanguine picture of many aspects of working-class life. It is true, he did not write much about the violence, the family pressures, the sexual inequality. But then, he was painting a picture not of reality, not even always of his own perception of reality, but a picture of the reality he wanted us to see. This is the nature of the Orwell/Blair dichotomy. 'Blair' had his private doubts. For example, in commenting on Graham Greene's work Orwell was highly critical of the implausibility of the plot of *Brighton Rock*. Pinkie, a small-time gangster engages in a moral dialogue with his 'still more limited' girlfriend, who neverthless is able to distinguish between the moral categories of good and evil, right and wrong. It is simply incredible, says Orwell, that 'the most brutish, stupid person can, merely by having been brought up a Catholic, be capable of great intellectual sublety'.[34] Orwell's guard is down here. He has shown us his own picture of reality (coloured by a streak of anti-Catholicism) by mistake and it is not a reality he wishes us to see too often. After all, if being brought up a Catholic does not help, why should being brought up in the working class be any different? In short, Orwell may or may not have 'got it wrong' but he was not naive: he was a propagandist. Generally speaking, we have to take it on trust that Orwell discovered what he believed to be moral values of great social and political importance among the better-off working class, so important that he gave his life to promoting them. 'Blair' may have had his doubts, but 'Orwell' kept the lid on them. Moreover, if these values of decency and justice have been eroded by socio-economic and cultural change, all the more important to make use of them while they still exist.

It will not do to pass over an obvious point concerning the moral values of the powerless by which Orwell set such store. If the Christian story is historically and theologically accurate, then the spirit which governs the universe chose to manifest itself in the son of a carpenter, in precisely the kind of family about which Orwell wrote. The crucial importance of this point hardly needs to be laboured. But suppose the story is largely myth? Then something even stranger and almost as momentous has occurred: the human spirit has chosen to create as one of its greatest heroes a moral teacher from among the powerless. In either case, the moral code constructed among the powerless was to prove tenacious enough to outlive the mighty Roman empire, which had sought to suppress it for over one thousand years.

Even so, it is still appropriate to ask whether Orwellism has any relevance for British socialism today. In the last decade of this century socialism, the dominant world ideology of the century, is almost everywhere in sharp decline. Not only have the highly centralised economies of the old Soviet Union and Eastern Europe collapsed, but the political legitimacy of those systems has been exposed as fraudulent; corrupt regimes supported by terror have fallen to almost unanimous popular acclaim. Doubtless, as new governments fail to solve the massive problems caused by decades of inefficient distribution and bureaucratic corruption, there will be a nostalgia for the old order and it is by no means impossible that some new forms of state socialism will emerge. They are unlikely to be any more successful or, in the long run, more popular than their predecessors. Moreover the economies of a number of countries in the Third World with single-party socialist systems appear to be in sharp decline to the extent that the future of many seems to be in doubt. As far as Britain is concerned, socialism, as represented by the Labour party, has fared little better. The rise of the party in the early years of this century was nothing less than meteoric. Until 1914 its existence as an independent party was in considerable doubt. In 1918, it produced a constitution setting out the socialist beliefs with which it proposed to confront the two major parties. Within six years Labour formed its first administration. Almost seventy years have passed since then, and during that time Britain has had only two Labour administrations with working majorities. If that were not in itself indictment enough of socialism in Britain, then we must also consider the retreat from its original socialist principles which the Labour party undertook following its third consecutive electoral defeat in 1987. Indeed, within ten years of its demise as a reforming socialist government (1945–50), the Labour party sought to rid itself of the commitment to nationalisation, the central plank of its socialist programme. Kinnock was a long way from being the first Labour leader to regard this aspect of socialism as an electoral liability. Is socialism in its death-throes and if so, is any question about the current relevance of Orwellism simply an anachronism?

Perhaps we should begin by briefly examining the reasons behind the decline of socialism in Britain. It would be doing no grave injustice to the complexity of the question to concentrate on the nature of socialist ideology and to tease out two dominant but separate traditions that have, with others, helped to shape that ideology since the early days of British socialism.[35]

Until the bitter disputes which bedevilled the Labour party from its electoral defeat in 1979 through to the early 1990s, there could be little doubt that socialism was a dominant ideology in Britain: indeed there was little competition, for the Conservatives used to claim apologetically that conservatism was not so much an ideology as an attitude of mind. Socialism, by contrast, claimed to be coherent and certain. True, such-and-such a Labour politician could be criticised for not really being a socialist but at least we knew, or thought we knew, what that meant. Nowadays we cannot be so sure. In fact, if we examine the development of socialism carefully we discover that nobody ever was so sure; indeed a whole industry grew up around the definition and redefinition of socialism.

What all seemed to agree on was the central importance of equality. There was disagreement, however, in the kind of equality to be aimed at and the manner in which it was to be achieved. Those we might group together, for the sake of simplicity, as fundamentalist socialists endorsed a programme seeking to create equality by abolishing capitalism through public ownership. The aim was to break up the existing state, not necessarily by violence, and to reconstitute it so that all its assets were communally owned and equally distributed. The social democrat on the other hand (again a distillation used here historically and not referring to the 1980s party of that name) was chiefly concerned to create equality by alleviating poverty. This aspiration stemmed from a humane concern for the underprivileged, but entailed nothing so ambitious as the reconstitution of social relations. So much for methods, but what about the nature of equality? Equality may be taken to refer to specific material conditions. Income, education, health, housing, for example, should be available to all in equal measure. Equality might also be taken to refer to power. Each person ought to have an equal say in the running of affairs. Now the Fabians, as we have seen, were perfectly convinced that the underprivileged were incapable of assisting in the running of a state in which power was shared equally: Fabians believed that the state should be controlled, in the interests of all, by a scientifically trained élite, a Platonic guardian class. We might refer to this as the scientific socialist tradition. Others among the early socialists, for example the Socialist League and its founder William Morris, favoured the equal sharing of power. These may be referred to as moralistic socialists, because their belief that men and women should control their own lives as much as possible constituted a moral position. So the moralistic tradition sought to allow the widest scope for individuals to take part in decisions affecting their lives, holding that this could only be done in a fundamentally restructured society.[36]

It is possible then, for the purposes of this analysis, to speak of four main kinds of socialism: scientific and moralistic fundamentalism, and scientific and moralistic social democracy. In fact, because the social democrats were less ambitious in their objectives and less ideological in their nature, differences between the two strands of social democracy could for the most part be ignored. In short, from its earliest days British socialism has represented an alliance between the social democrats and the fundamentalists, the latter subdivided between the moralistic and scientific traditions. Nor are these tensions unique to British socialism: indeed, according to R. N. Berki, socialism is never and nowhere a 'single thing, but a range, an area, an open texture, a self-contradiction'.[37] Not surprising, then, to find that socialism has lost its way; not surprising that the British Labour party is as divided today as ever about its relationship to 'socialism', with survey findings indicating that party activists have little in common with the principal policy aspirations of the leadership, though all recognise the importance of winning power.[38]

Following the electoral defeat of 1987 a series of personal views by leading party figures was published which indicated that tensions within the party were alive and well. Social democrats within the party, referred to disparagingly by union leader Ron Todd as 'filofax socialists', were concerned that fundamentalists had condemned the party to successive electoral defeats by projecting an antiquated electoral image. For the fundamentalists the problem has been exactly the opposite of this: if only the party would espouse true socialism and not trim it, it would gain wider electoral support. David Blunkett wanted the party to emphasise the values and morality of libertarian and democratic socialism and believed that it should reject the idea that socialism meant 'having state or local bureaucrats telling you what to do'.[39] Bryan Gould and Michael Meacher recognised that a victory at the polls meant appealing to the 'high-tech salariat and the new working class who live in the South'; their emphasis was not on repackaging traditional socialist policies but on producing a set of policies that the electorate would buy.[40] Indeed the very terminology used, redolent of that which coloured Labour's full-scale policy review, is suggestive of a thorough going market-led approach which was anathema to fundamentalists. For these, the great requirement for the party was, as always, to stand by the trade unions and to reassert its socialist faith, to recognise 'whose side we are on when the struggles begin outside parliament' because 'vigorous – and possibly violent – resistance to renewed attacks on trade unions and democracy' might prove necessary.[41]

There is, however, more to be said about the current problems of the party than that they reflect traditional divisions. Two other important factors need to be mentioned. First the decline of institutionalised Christianity. In its earlier days the Labour movement was frequently associated with a moral system, that of non-conformist and Low Church Christianity, which helped to shape the lives of many ordinary people. The Clarion movement, for example, brought together socialism and non-conformity with its Clarion church choirs, Sunday schools, brass and silver bands, cycling clubs, and holiday camps in the North of England. Indeed it has been truly said that the British Labour movement owes more to Methodism than to Marxism. Nowadays, by contrast, a critic can write: 'That the Left is irrelevant to the mainstream of British social life is shown by its concentration on fringe issues and minority groups':[42] Labour was being criticised as merely a conventicle of the dispossessed. In earlier times the conscience of a Judaeo-Christian culture might not have allowed such concerns to be marginalised in this way. In short, the moral climate in which the Labour party grew and flourished seems to have changed.

The second factor is the eclipse of scientific socialism. When Shaw and his fellow Fabians fired their shafts they aimed principally at men of influence, believing that socialism was such common sense that it was necessary only to argue its case properly for wise men to become convinced. After all, how could a state controlled amateurishly by the wealthy in their own interests (with all the potential for discontent that this entailed) be more successful from anybody's point of view than a planned society controlled in the interests of all by a specially trained élite? Needless to say, the Fabians and fellow scientific socialists did not persuade the majority of businessmen or indeed civil servants, but they were on the winning side in the Labour party: for a variety of reasons, practical as well as ideological, the idea of socialism became synonymous with state socialism – 'Leviathan moralised'.[43] It is undeniable that things have not worked out as the Fabians and others envisaged. Nationalisation has not, on the whole, been an economic success, nor has it given to ordinary workers a sense of identity with the businesses they 'own'.

Taking these factors together we find that the cutting edge of the ideology of socialism has been dulled, its self-confidence dispelled. The world in which it grew up and flourished has changed, in no small measure as a consequence of its own endeavours.

How is Labour to respond? Shorn of its moralistic and scientific certainties, the tensions within the party seem unresolvable. On the one hand social democrats would probably agree with Austin Mitchell that 'talking of socialism we are talking to ourselves'; on the other, the fundamentalists have no enthusiasm for being led to an unrecognisable promised land by 'a market consultant beating the drum and an advertising consultant carrying the banner'.[44]

What cemented the party in the past was its commitment to the working class; unlike its opponents the Labour party has been unashamed to declare its class allegiance. No doubt many have always seen the party as *more* than a working-class party, but it has usually acknowledged itself to be *at least* that. In the inter-war years approximately 75 per cent of the parliamentary Labour party had attended only elementary school; when Labour was last in office, by contrast, the equivalent figure was 16 per cent with no fewer than 56 per cent having been educated at university. In general terms the party in parliament has become less a party of workers, more a party of professionals (especially communicators). The party leadership, moreover, amongst whom workers were once conspicuous, is now almost monopolised by the professions – though some come from working-class backgrounds. What is true of the parliamentary party is true of constituency associations to an increasing extent, so that the present Labour movement is, at most, a movement not of but on behalf of the working class. Not surprisingly the working class has become increasingly disaffected. In recent years not only has the traditionally solid social structure of the working class changed significantly, but in many respects the party is seen to have pursued policies not in the working-class interest. Moreover, the party has intentionally sought to transform its working-class image. Some years ago the party abandoned the singing of 'The Red Flag' at the conclusion of party conferences presumably because of its offensively radical-socialist connotations and replaced it with the equally resonant but less revolutionary 'Auld Lang Syne'. Now 'The Red Flag' is back, and what is more, those on the platform have learned the words. This is not because the party has reasserted its radicalism: in fact the opposite. It is because that kind of radicalism has become part of history and its anthem a piece of harmless pantomime nostalgia.

The problems set out here help in part to explain the general electoral decline of the party since Attlee. If the party is to win power again, to be successful in government and to sustain itself as a party of regular government – which it has managed to do only during one brief period in its history, from 1964 to 1979 – it needs to be much clearer as to what it stands for. The difficulty of this task is amply illustrated by recent Fabian pamphlets by two socialist intellectuals, Raymond Plant[45] and Bernard Crick.[46] Plant acknowledges that Labour's welfare provision has not succeeded but argues that the party must defend collective and public welfare provision on moral and efficiency grounds, by emphasising community and not central values; he calls his position democratic equality. Crick moves more towards Shaw's position – socialism requires equality of income. Plant will not accept this. He follows the Rawlsian case that some inequalities benefit the whole of society and therefore it is irrational to insist upon equality in such circumstances. There is a familiar ring to the argument and it indicates that Labour's future might well be dogged by the same divisions that have helped to shape its past.

And now back to Orwellism. If there was one popular socialist thinker who predicted the failure of centralised, scientific socialism it was Orwell: he was utterly convinced that it would lapse into totalitarianism. Orwell would be classified as a moralistic socialist, but since he himself was so much against ideologies and 'isms' he ought not to be classified at all. He argued for an approach which emphasised the interests of ordinary people. He despised the notion of an intellectual class acting in the interests of the people; only the people could do that. Though he had a set of specific suggestions for the incoming Labour government in 1945, there is no blueprint for the future in Orwell's writings to which Labour party thinkers may turn today for guidance. Yet that it precisely Orwell's relevance for the Labour party in today's Britain. Orwellism is pragmatic, but it is pragmatic within a framework provided by the interests of ordinary people.

If a party wishes to base its policies upon the values and hopes of ordinary people, it can only do so by actually considering these values and asking what these hopes are, and by involving people in seeking their fulfilment. Of course, they will not always be capable of being fulfilled; Orwell recognised that politics was often about choosing the lesser of two evils, but the more ordinary people were involved in these decisions, the less likely morally unacceptable decisions were to be made. It is difficult to believe, for example, that working-class communities would have chosen to rehouse themselves in high-rise estates, thereby destroying themselves. If the Labour party were to pay heed to Orwell it would do what it has significantly failed to do in the past: trust the people and not the experts.

This would require a genuine commitment to making the policy processes accessible to ordinary people. For a start it means a socialist discourse not dominated by jargon. It was Orwell who recognised, as Steiner pointed out, that to abuse, inflate or falsify the meaning of words it to devalue the political process. Political sanity and the ability of a community to view and communicate issues are clearly dependent upon the integrity of syntax . . . The fight for meaningful speech is a fight for moral and political life.[47]

It is not only lawyers and civil servants who have created languages to which the powerless have no access; left-wing political discourse is frequently impenetrable.

It follows from this that political structures must also be made accessible. As long as politics is a specialised activity conducted centrally by groups claiming expertise, ordinary people will not be interested, as Anthony Crosland depairingly noted in his seminal work *The Future of Socialism*. Oscar Wilde, as was his manner, put the issue rather more succinctly: the problem with socialism, he wrote, was that it took too many evenings. The need to strengthen the relationship between the values and aspirations of ordinary people and the Labour party is greater today than ever it was, for socialism's soul, as Orwell said, is to be found in the values of ordinary people. The decline of institutional Christianity should not obscure the fact that those values are, according to Orwell, basically Judaeo-Christian, though they have much in common with the values of other religious communities in this country.

As long as people are bound together in an oppressive relationship, as long as there is a potential for one group to dominate, then it will do so. Moreover, revolutions, which are about the conquest of power, will only replace one power-group with another. There may follow a temporary respite 'such as a sick man gets by turning over in bed', but so long as the *structure* of power is not dismantled, the innate instinct to power will remain a threat, forever waiting the opportunity to slip its lead. The more power is diffused, the more power structures are broken up, the more difficult it becomes for them to be manipulated. To its cost, Labour has traditionally operated in exactly the opposite way. Its programme of nationalisation created monopoly services that dominated the lives of ordinary people. None believed that those services belonged to them: quite the reverse. In the Midlands several years ago a woman put her head in a gas oven because she had received (in error) a gas bill twenty times greater than normal. Did she believe that the nationalised British Gas belonged to her? It was Chesterton who argued that the great irrationality of socialism was to believe that power in capitalist society was held by too few hands, and then to propose putting it into fewer hands – those of socialist politicians. From Orwell's perspective, if socialism is truly to represent ordinary people, then it must encourage the emergence of structures of power which, though they might have a national framework and a central coordinating capacity, will nonetheless be diffused and have a truly local, community-based aspect. Moreover, socialism must promote among its leaders and administrators a Confucian conquest of the desire for power and mastery – what Orwell and Koestler called 'the will not to will'. Only then, Orwell believes, might socialism by-pass the major problems of politics hitherto: that of combining power with righteousness. It is only by dispersing and demystifying power that socialism can rid itself of the threat of managerial despotism and the menace of Big Brother; only by dispersing and demystifying power that it may be made accessible to ordinary people.

Is Orwellism just the wishful thinking of a middle-class humanitarian? Vaclav Havel, once Czechoslovakia's most celebrated dissident playwright, and now its first democratically elected president since World War Two, wrote an essay in 1978 called 'The Power of the Powerless',[48] which circulated only privately. In it he depicted life in his own nation as a world much like Oceania, a dictatorship in which 'the centre of power is the centre of truth'. He examines the nature of the dominant ideology (which, like Orwell, he sees as a 'means' and not an 'end'), describing it as hypocrisy and lies. When he gives examples we recogise it immediately for Orwell's doublethink: government by bureaucracy is popular government, the working class is enslaved in the name of the working class, the destruction of individual liberty is ultimate freedom, arbitrary power is called the legal code, the expansion of empire is called support for the oppressed, and so on. 'Because the regime is captive to its own lies, it must falsify everything. It falsifies the past. It falsifies the present, and it falsifies the future.' Havel defined ideology as 'the interpretation of reality by the power structure', so that reality does not shape theory, but exactly the reverse.

Yet under the surface of this life of lies there sleeps what Havel calls the openness to truth. The power of truth is only a potential power, but it exists, hidden, through the whole of society. This potential power 'does not participate in any direct struggle for power; rather it makes its presence felt in the obscure arena of being itself'. Yet it takes only one small boy to cry out that the Emperor has no clothes and an entire political edifice can be brought down. This, says Havel, is why the Soviets expelled Solzhenitsyn – openness must be silenced. This potential for popular power is described by Havel as 'pre-political' and, unlike Orwell, he locates it with the intelligentsia as well as the workers. This difference can be explained simply. Havel's intelligentsia were not a pampered cosmopolitan group such as Orwell despised but dissidents whose stand threatened their very liberty and life. Yet Havel makes it clear that workers who are simply trying to do their job well are potential enemies of the Party too because they are bound inevitably to fall foul of the bureaucracy.

Also like Orwell, Havel's arguments have a religious foundation. While he acknowledges the importance of religion in building a base to his moral system, so as to create a 'second culture' and eventually a 'parallel polis', he is reticent about using the word 'God'. Heinrich Böll has written that this reticence reflects a 'courtesy [which] no longer addresses God with the name that has been trampled underfoot by politicians'.[49] Yet he quotes Havel as acknowledging that 'should God not exist in that place which I am trying to define then all will appear to be nothing more than some form of abstract construction or subterfuge'. It is difficult not to believe that, at least privately, Orwell would have accepted the primacy of Havel's Christ, whose name Havel would not mention for fear of 'those Christian drummer boys, representing their explosive form of Chistianity [who would] lay their hands on it'.[50]

Like Orwell, Havel knows the overriding importance of a moral code:

> If a better economic and political model is to be created, then perhaps more than ever it must derive from profound existential and moral changes in society . . . a better system will not automatically ensure a better life. In fact the opposite is true; only by creating a better life can a better system be developed.

The similarity with Orwell and indeed Dickens is very close, but what Havel sought to change was the nature of communism, not capitalism. It must not be thought that Havel warmed much towards Western capitalist democracy, for he saw communism as 'a kind of warning to the West, revealing its own latent tendencies'. He finds no evidence of human rediscovery in 'the omnipresent dictatorship of consumption, production, advertising, commerce, consumer culture'. Indeed the changes he seeks clearly reflect not capitalism but Orwellism.

> There can and must be structures that are open, dynamic and small; beyond a certain point, human ties like personal trust and personal responsibility cannot work ... Any accumulation of power whatsoever ... should be profoundly alien ... They would be structures not in the sense of organisations or institutions, but like a community.

As for the economic structure, Havel strives for 'what all the theorists of socialism have dreamed about, that is, the genuine participation of workers in the economic decision-making'. Havel refers to his version of Orwellism as post-democratic theory, the consequence of an 'existential revolution'.

The collapse of communism in Czechoslovakia does not imply the establishment of post-democracy. Havel recognised in the workers and the dissident intellectuals the moral force necessary for its establishment, but acknowledged, also, that this force might be dissipated with the end of the repression of the communist system. Yet like Orwell he remains hopeful. 'What if [the "bright future"] has been here for a long time already, and only our own blindness and weakness has prevented us from seeing it around us and within us, and kept us from developing it?'

If the British Labour party is concerned to regain its sense of mission (what commentators have called the moral high ground), its thinkers might benefit from a reconsideration of the writings of George Orwell. They might conclude that socialism has been undone by ideology, as Orwell said it would be; that what it needs, perhaps, is an Orwellian code of conduct, a framework of values based upon the pillars of decency and justice. If Labour is to regain its belief in the wisdom of a planned economy – and the problems to be faced as a consequence of global environmental deterioration hardly seem amenable to market-based solutions – then its thinkers might do well to consider the structures through which such planning might be undertaken. Socialists can never build an equal and just society compatible with individual freedom unless 'the concept of right and wrong is restored to politics',[51] because ordinary people will have to *believe* in socialism. The forces that shape the world, said Orwell, spring from emotions, not ideologies or scientific principles,[52] and only that belief, nurtured in Havel's community-based structures of power, will make socialism work.

A non-ideological socialism seems at first a contradiction in terms, but not if it were firmly based upon Orwellian values. In principle, such a socialism would find no difficulty in cooperating with other parties which claimed to share these values so as to achieve parliamentary power. But Orwellian and Havellian values would have to provide the touchstone for any such arrangement.

In the harsh world of Britain in the 1990s a code of political conduct has developed which declares that there is no such thing as society. Labour seems to have been caught on the Morton's fork of its traditional statist socialism and a form of 'me-tooism' in which pleasant men and women in suits persuade bankers and businessmen that they have nothing to fear. Neither seems to offer an appropriate programme of action. If it is to become more than an alternative capitalist party, Labour ought surely to defend a planned economy which seeks to safeguard the environment and which offers hope of a caring society which would seek to safeguard the interests of the dispossessed through the operation of community-based structures of power. If the majority of voters reject such a programme, properly presented, then indeed there is no future for the politics of decency. Yet the huge amounts of money raised by charities in recent years suggest that ordinary people have well-developed awareness and compassion.

Orwellism could not claim to provide a blueprint for the future policy programme of a Labour government, nor indeed any guarantee of electoral success, but the prospect of a world in which Orwellian and Havellian values had withered away entirely is a distressing one: a code of political conduct espousing the 'politics of decency' was never more needed .

References

Preface

1 See Julian Symons' review of John Rodden's *The Politics of Literary Reputations: The Making and Claiming of St George Orwell* in the *London Review of Books*, 9 November 1989.

Chapter 1

1 Michael Shelden, *Orwell: The Authorised Biography*, Heinemann, 1991, pp. 13–5.
2 See Stephen Wadhams, *Remembering Orwell*, Penguin, 1984, ch. 1.
3 Written in 1947 and to be found in *The Collected Essays, Journalism and Letters (CEJL)* 4, Secker and Warburg, 1968, pp. 330–69.
4 Cyril Connolly, *The Enemies of Promise*, Routledge and Kegan Paul, 1938, p.160.
5 Peter Stansky and William Abrahams, *The Unknown Orwell*, Constable, 1972, p. 39.
6 Quoted in Wadhams, 1984, p.10.
7 Sir John Grostian, in Bernard Crick, *George Orwell: A Life*, Secker and Warburg, 1980, p. 29.
8 Henry Longhurst, *My Life and Soft Times*, Cassell, 1972, p. 26.
9 Ibid., p. 37.
10 Quoted in Wadhams, 1984, p. 13; see also Jacintha Buddicom, 'The Young Eric', in Miriam Gross (ed.), *The World of George Orwell*, Weidenfeld and Nicolson, 1971.
11 Jacintha Buddicom, *Eric and Us*, Leslie Frewin, 1974, p. 53.
12 Stansky and Abrahams, 1972.
13 Crick, p. 46.
14 Buddicom, 1974.
15 Stansky and Abrahams, *op.cit.*, p. 81
16 See Crick, 1980, ch. 4.
17 Sir Roger Mynors, in Wadhams, 1984, p. 19.
18 Shelden, 1991, pp. 75–8.
19 See Crick, 1980, p. 63.
20 Wadhams, 1984, p. 21.
21 Jeffrey Meyers, *George Orwell: The Critical Heritage*, Routledge, 1975, p. 378.
22 Crick, 1980, pp. 96–8.
23 Maun Htin Aung, in ibid., p. 96.
24 Harold Acton, *Memoirs of an Aesthete*, Methuen, 1970, p. 152.
25 Shelden, 1991, pp. 109–10.
26 Buddicom, 1974, pp. 143–4.

27 Shelden, 1991, p. 105.
28 R. A. Lee, *Orwell's Fiction*, University of Notre Dame Press, 1969, p. 3.
29 *Burmese Days*, Penguin, 1969, p. 23.
30 Ibid., p. 24.
31 Ibid., p. 28.
32 Ibid., p. 29.
33 Ibid., p. 37.
34 Ibid., p. 66.
35 Lee, 1969, p. xiii.
36 BBC interview in Shelden, 1991, p. 203.
37 Ibid., p. 33.
38 See Peter Lewis, *George Orwell*, Heinemann, 1981, p. 35.
39 K. Aldritt, *The Making of George Orwell*, Edward Arnold, 1969, p. 109.
40 Raymond Williams, *Orwell*, Fontana, 1971, p. 19.

Chapter 2
1 Bernard Crick, *George Orwell: A Life*, Secker and Warburg, 1981, p. 106.
2 *Road to Wigan Pier*, Harmondsworth, Penguin, 1963, pp. 149–50.
3 Crick, 1981, p. 111.
4 *CEJL* 1, p. 493.
5 Crick, 1981, p. 112.
6 Ibid., p. 118.
7 Ibid.
8 Raymond Williams, *Orwell*, Fontana, 1971, p. 52.
9 Crick, 1981, p. 129.
10 Ibid., p. 127.
11 *CEJL* 1, pp. 63–4.
12 *CEJL* 1, p. 155.
13 'The Proletarian Writer', *CEJL* 2, pp. 39–40.
14 *CEJL* 1, p. 81.
15 Ibid., p. 103.
16 Crick, 1981, p. 142.
17 Ibid.
18 *CEJL* 1, pp. 27–8.
19 *CEJL* 1, pp. 154–6.
20 In a letter to his friend Dennis Collings, Orwell wrote about huge notices he had seen in a Bible Society window advertising the cheapest Roman Catholic bibles at 5/6d and the cheapest Protestant bible at 1/-. 'So long as that spirit is in the land we are safe from the RCs'. (*CEJL* 1, p. 50.)
21 See Orwell's review of Jack Hilton's *Caliban Strikes*, *CEJL* 1, pp. 148–9.
22 Michael Shelden, *Orwell: The Authorised Biography*, Heinemann, 1991, p. 229.
23 Crick, 1981, pp. 143–4.
24 *Down and Out in Paris and London*, Penguin, 1969, p. 17.
25 Ibid., p. 14.
26 Ibid., p. 45.
27 Ibid., p. 46.
28 Ibid., p. 45.
29 Ibid., p. 69.

30 Lynette Hunter, *The Search for a Voice*, Open University Press, 1984.
31 *Weekend Telegraph*, 16 September 1989.
32 John Rodden, *The Making and Claiming of 'St George' Orwell*, Oxford University Press, 1989, p. 40.
33 *Down and Out*, pp. 146–7.
34 *A Clergyman's Daughter*, Penguin, 1964, pp. 14–5.
35 Ibid., p. 53.
36 Ibid., p. 220.
37 Ibid., p. 252.
38 Ibid., p. 259.
39 Lee, *Orwell's Fiction*, University of Notre Dame Press, 1969, p. 25.
40 *Clergyman's Daughter*, pp. 318–9.
41 *Keep the Aspidistra Flying*, Penguin, 1965, pp. 18–9.
42 Ibid., p. 102.
43 Ibid., p. 122.
44 Ibid., p. 49.
45 Ibid., p. 253.
46 See 'Reflections on Gandhi', *CEJL* 4, pp. 463–70.
47 *Scrutiny IX*, September 1940, in K. Aldritt, *The Making of George Orwell*, Edward Arnold, 1969, p. 19.
48 Compton Mckenzie, in Peter Lewis, *George Orwell*, Heinemann, 1981, p. 48.
49 Williams, 1971, pp. 46–9.
50 George Woodcock, *The Crystal Spirit*, Jonathan Cape, 1967, p. 104.

Chapter 3

1 Crick, *George Orwell: A Life*, Secker and Warburg, 1981, p.183.
2 Ibid., p. 184.
3 See Orwell's own account in 'The Road to Wigan Pier *Diary*' in *CEJL* 1, pp. 184–7.
4 See letter to Jack Common, *CEJL* 1, pp. 168–9.
5 See letter to Denys King-Farlow, *CEJL* 1, pp. 224–5.
6 Raymond Williams, *George Orwell*, Fontana, 1971, p. 23.
7 Harold Laski, *Left News*, March 1937, in Meyers, *The Critical Heritage*, Routledge, 1975, pp. 105–6.
8 Arnold Toynbee, *Encounter*, August 1959.
9 Walter Greenwood, *Tribune*, 12 March 1937.
10 Shelden, *Orwell: The Authorised Biography*, Heinemann, 1991, pp. 298–9.
11 Ibid., p. 295.
12 *CEJL* 1, p. 299.
13 A copy of the full text is to be found in Crick, 1981, p. 228.
14 Ibid., p. 229.
15 Letter to Geoffrey Gorer, *CEJL* 1, pp. 284–8.
16 Crick, 1981, p. 235.
17 Rodden, *The Making and Claiming of 'St George' Orwell*, Oxford University Press, 1989, p. 333.
18 Crick, 1981, p. 239.
19 Ibid., p. 245.
20 Shelden, 1991, p. 321.

21 *CEJL* 1, pp. 337–8.
22 Letter to Jack Common, *CEJL* 1, p. 357.
23 *CEJL* 1, pp. 380–8.
24 *CEJL* 1, p. 333.
25 William Steinhof, *Road to Nineteen Eighty-four*, Weidenfeld and Nicolson, 1975, p. 172.
26 Shelden, 1991, pp. 331–3.
27 Ibid., pp. 345–6.
28 Ibid., p. 12.
29 *CEJL* 1, pp. 394–8.
30 *The Road to Wigan Pier*, Penguin, 1963, p. 64.
31 Ibid., p. 68.
32 Ibid., p. 76.
33 Ibid., p. 113.
34 Ibid., p. 130.
35 Ibid., pp. 149–50.
36 Ibid., p. 156.
37 Ibid., p. 154.
38 Ibid., p. 189.
39 Ibid., p. 195.
40 Ibid., p. 202.
41 *Homage to Catalonia*, Penguin, 1962, pp. 8–9.
42 *CEJL* 1, p. 259.
43 *Homage*, 1962, p. 245.

Chapter 4

 1 'My Country, Right or Left', *CEJL* 1, pp. 535–41.
 2 Wartime Diary, *CEJL* 2, p. 347.
 3 Bernard Crick, *George Orwell: A Life*, Secker and Warburg, 1981, pp. 262–3.
 4 Ibid., p. 265.
 5 Cyril Connolly, *The Evening Colonnade*, London, Bruce and Watson, 1973, p. 382.
 6 *CEJL* 2, pp. 27–8.
 7 *Tribune*, December 20 1940.
 8 Crick, 1981, p. 271.
 9 Michael Shelden, *Orwell: The Authorised Biography*, Heinemann, 1991, p. 356.
10 Fredric Warburg, *All Authors Are Equal*, Hutchinson, 1973, pp. 37–9.
11 *The Observer*, 9 May 1943 and 15 October 1944, quoted in Crick, 1981, p. 272.
12 Ibid., p. 287.
13 Ibid., p. 306.
14 'As I Please', 31 January 1947, *CEJL* 4, pp. 278–9.
15 Letter to Gleb Struve, 17 February 1944, *CEJL* 3, pp. 95–6.
16 'Why I write', *CEJL* 1, p. 7.
17 Crick, 1981, p. 311.
18 Letter to Leonard Moore (his literary agent), 23 February 1946, *CEJL* 4, p. 110.
19 In the summer of 1940 Orwell had written: 'Thinking always of my island in the Hebrides, which I suppose I shall never possess or see.' (Wartime Diary, June 20th 1940, *CEJL* 2, pp. 350–3.

20 See Crick, 1981, pp. 328–9.
21 Shelden, 1991, p. 433.
22 Crick, 1981, p. 334.
23 Shelden, 1991, pp. 445–6.
24 Crick, 1981, pp. 335–6.
25 Ibid., p. 341.
26 *Homage to Catalonia*, Penguin, 1962, p. 59.
27 Arthur Koestler, *Darkness at Noon*, Penguin, 1969, pp. 81–133, *passim*.
28 *Homage*, p. 99.
29 *CEJL* 4, p. 7.
30 An excellent example of the conflict between ends and means is explored in Aldous Huxley's *Point Counter Point*, Penguin, 1972, following the assassination of the fascist leader Everard Webley. See pp. 390–5.
31 *Homage*, p. 59.
32 *CEJL 1*, p. 366.
33 G. K. Chesterton, *Heretics*, John Lane, 1928, *passim*.
34 William Morris, *News from Nowhere*, Lawrence & Wishart, 1973, ch. XVII.
35 *Homage*, p. 234.
36 Letter to Cyril Connolly dated 8 June 1937, *CEJL* 1, pp. 280–2.
37 *CEJL* 3, p. 78.
38 *CEJL* 2, p. 9.
39 'London letter' to *Partisan Review*, *CEJL* 2, p. 230.
40 *CEJL* 2, p. 341.
41 *CEJL* 2, p. 227.
42 *CEJL* 3, p. 294.
43 *CEJL* 1, p. 283.
44 Letter to Geoffrey Gorer, 15 September 1937, *CEJL* 1, pp. 280–2.
45 Shelden, 1991, p. 407.
46 *CEJL* 2, p. 176.
47 H. M. Hyndman, *Record of an Adventurous Life*, Macmillan, 1911, p. 432.
48 *CEJL* 3, p. 244.

Chapter 5

1 *CEJL* 4, p. 447.
2 See Crick, *George Orwell: A Life,* Secker and Warburg, 1981, p. 345.
3 *CEJL* 4, pp. 145–6.
4 *CEJL* 4, p. 378.
5 *CEJL* 4, pp. 329–30.
6 See Anthony West, 'George Orwell', in *Principles and Persuasions*, Eyre and Spottiswoode, 1958, pp. 150–9.
7 Crick, 1981, pp. 364–5.
8 *CEJL* 4, p. 404.
9 *CEJL* 4, p. 438.
10 Crick, 1981, p. 383.
11 *CEJL* 4, p. 475.
12 *CEJL* 4, p. 515.
13 Crick, 1981, p. 391.
14 G. Woodcock, *The Crystal Spirit*, Jonathan Cape, 1967, p. 166.

15 *CEJL* 4, pp. 160–81.
16 *CEJL* 1, pp. 332–4.
17 See C. M. Joad (ed.), *Shaw and Society*, Odhams, 1953, p. 41.
18 George Bernard Shaw, *The Simple Truth About Socialism*, 1912 (L. Crompton, *The Road to Equality*, Beacon Press, 1971, p. 163).
19 In A. Cappelow, *Shaw – "The Chucker Out" – A Biographical Exposition and Critique*, Allen and Unwin, 1969, p. 199.
20 Bernard Shaw, *The Simple Truth About Socialism* in Crompton, 1971, p. 183.
21 Gollo Mann, *Frankfürter Rundschau*, 5 November 1949, in Meyers, *The Critical Heritage*, Routledge, 1975, pp. 277–81.
22 *CEJL* 1, p. 35.
23 Letter to Brenda Salkeld, 1932, *CEJL* 1, p. 119.
24 Raymond Williams, *Orwell*, Fontana, 1971.
25 *Nineteen Eighty-four*, Penguin, 1960, p. 211.
26 Ibid., p. 214.
27 George Kateb, 'The Road to Nineteen Eighty-four', *Political Science Quarterly* 4, 1966, pp. 565–81.
28 Hannah Arendt, *The Origins of Totalitarianism*, Harcourt Brace Jovanovich, 1973.
29 Karl Popper, *The Open Society and its Enemies*, 2, Routledge, 1968.
30 Isaac Deutscher, 'The Mysticism of Cruelty', in *Heretics and Renegades*, Hamish Hamilton, 1955.
31 'Wells, Hitler and the world state', *CEJL* 2, pp. 139–45.
32 Ibid., pp. 214–5.
33 Arendt, 1973, p. 451.
34 *CEJL* 1, pp. 375–6.
35 William Steinhof, *Road to Nineteen Eighty-four*, Weidenfeld and Nicolson, 1975, p. 172.
36 See 'The Prevention of Literature', *CEJL* 4, p. 61.
37 *CEJL* 1, p. 175.
38 Patrick Reilly, *George Orwell, The Age's Adversary*, Macmillan, 1986, p. 46.
39 *CEJL* 3, p. 87.
40 Popper, 1968, ii, p. 66.
41 Arendt, 1973, p. 400.
42 Milan Kundera, *The Book of Laughter and Forgetting*, Penguin, 1983. This book begins with a picture of senior Czech figures appearing before a crowd in Prague. It is snowing and the leader has not hat. His solicitous lieutenant loans him his own fur hat. Hundreds of thousands of copies of the ensuing photograph were issued. Four years later the lieutenant was hanged for treason. 'The propaganda section immediately airbrushed him out of history, and, obviously, out of all the photographs as well. All that remains of Clemantis [the lieutenant] is the cap on Gottwald's [the leader's] head.' (p. 3.)
43 In *The Social Crisis of our Time* (William Hodge & Co., 1950) Wilhelm Röpke also emphasised the importance of family life in preserving the kind of personal values which make democracy feasible. More than thirty years later Mrs Thatcher set up the Family Unit in her Cabinet because she feared the decline of these values.
44 *CEJL* 4, p.91.

45 *Nineteen Eighty-four*, p. 46.
46 Kundera, 1983, p. 159.
47 Ibid., p. 157.
48 *Nineteen Eighty-four*, p. 103.
49 Irving Howe, 'History of nightmare in politics', *Politics and the Novel*, Horizon, 1957.
50 See 'The Lion and the Unicorn', *CEJL* 2, pp. 56–109.
51 'As I please', 28 April 1944, *CEJL* 3, pp. 131–4.
52 Chris Small, *The Road to Miniluv*, Gollancz, 1975, *passim*.
53 Reilly, 1986, p. 294.

Chapter 6

1 In *The Crystal Spirit*, Jonathan Cape, 1967. The author refers to Orwell as a 'noticeably ambivalent anarchist' (p. 28).
2 He did, after all, join the Trotskyist POUM in Spain. Eliot, moreover, considered him a Trotskyist and Wells referred to him as 'that Trotskyite with the big feet'.
3 This was his own insistent claim after 1936.
4 See *The Lion and the Unicorn* for example.
5 A commonly-held communist view especially prevalent, it will be remembered, after the Spanish civil war.
6 For example, Alan Sandison, *George Orwell After 1984*, Macmillan, 1986.
7 Raymond Williams, *George Orwell*, Fontana, 1971, pp. 77–81.
8 See David Kuball, *Outside the Whale: George Orwell's Art and Politics*, University of Notre Dame Press, 1972, p. 49.
9 See Lionel Trilling, 'George Orwell and the Politics of Truth' in *The Opposing Self*, 1955, pp. 150–9.
10 Richard Rees, *Fugitive From the Camp of Victory*, Secker and Warburg, 1961, p. 147.
11 *CEJL* 1, p. 228.
12 Dietrich Bonhoeffer, *Ethics*, Fontana, 1968, pp. 85–6.
13 *CEJL* 2, p. 15.
14 Review of *Tropic of Cancer*, *CEJL* 1, pp. 154–6.
15 *CEJL* 1, pp. 529–32.
16 *Spectator* 16 January 1971, p. 87.
17 Rodden, *The Making and Claiming of 'St.George' Orwell*, Oxford University Press, 1989, p. 184.
18 Christopher Hollis, *A Study of George Orwell*, Hollis and Carter, 1956, p. 86.
19 *CEJL* 3, p. 100.
20 Hollis, 1956.
21 *CEJL* 3, pp. 234–44.
22 *CEJL* 1, pp. 529–32.
23 *CEJL* 3, p. 103.
24 The clearest exposition of Orwell's thought on this is to be found in his *The English People*, *CEJL* 3, pp. 1–37.
25 *CEJL* 2, pp. 155–64.
26 Donald McGill was a collective pen-name for the designers of a set of postcards which almost invariably depicted fat middle-aged women, hen-pecked husbands

and vivacious girls in a variety of predictable holiday situations.
27 Review of *Caliban Shrieks* by Jack Hilton, *CEJL* 1, pp. 148–50.
28 Samuel Hynes (ed.), *Twentieth-Century Interpretations of Nineteen Eighty-four*, Prentice Hall, 1971, p. 3.
29 *The Road to Wigan Pier*, Penguin, 1962, p. 157.
30 *Nineteen Eighty-four*, Penguin, 1960, pp. 58–9.
31 Ibid.
32 Rodden, 1989, p. 173.
33 C. C. O'Brien, *Writers and Politics*, Chatto and Windus, 1965, pp. 32–3.
34 *CEJL* 4, p. 442.
35 I have set out a fuller account of this in *British Party System*, Blackwells, 1989, ch. 5.
36 The significance of this debate is developed in Stephen Ingle, 'Socialist man: William Morris and Bernard Shaw', in B. Parekh (ed.), *Concepts of Socialism*, Croom Helm, 1975.
37 See R. N. Berki, *Socialism*, Dent, 1975, *passim*.
38 Patrick Seyd *et al.*, 'Labour Reorganisation down at the Grassroots', paper presented to the PSA Specialist Group on parties and elections, September 1990.
39 *Independent*, 7 July 1987.
40 *Independent*, 9 July 1987.
41 *Independent*, 14 July 1987.
42 Anthony Hartley, *Sunday Times*, 27 July 1987.
43 Ibid.
44 *Sunday Times*, 13 September 1987.
45 Raymond Plant, *Equality, Markets and the State*, Fabian Tract 494, 1984, and *Citizenship, Rights and Socialism*, Fabian Tract 531, 1988.
46 Bernard Crick, *Socialist Values and Time*, Fabian Tract 495, 1984.
47 George Steiner, in *The Critical Heritage*, ed. Meyers Routledge, 1975, pp. 139–51.
48 Vaclav Havel, 'The power of the powerless', in J. Vladislav, *Vaclav Havel or Living from Truth*, Faber and Faber, 1987, pp. 36–122.
49 Heinrich Böll, 'Courtesy towards God', ibid., pp. 204–12.
50 Ibid.
51 *CEJL* 3, p. 119.
52 *CEJL* 2, p. 141.

Index

Adelphi, 46
Amnesty International, 84
Anglicanism, Orwell's attachment
  to, 21–3, 29, 30–1, 39
Animal Farm, 63, 64, 65, 68,
  76–82, 83, 107, 115–16
Archbishop of Canterbury, 90
Arendt, Hannah, 97
'Art of Donald McGill', 111
Astor, David, 62, 65, 88, 89, 90,
  91
Attlee, Clement (Lord), 74, 86,
  127
Auden, W. H., 109
Ayer, A. J., 66

Barnhill, Jura, Orwell's move to,
  85
BBC, Orwell working for, 61–2
Bellow, Saul, *Mr Sammler's Planet*,
  95
Berki, R. N., on socialism, 124–5
Bevan, Aneurin, 85
Blair, Avril, 61, 84, 85, 86, 88, 89,
  90, 91
Blair, Eileen, née O'Shaughnessy,
  24, 41–2, 45, 58, 60, 64
  illness and death, 66–7
Blair, Ida Mabel, née Limouzin, 1,
  61
Blair, Marjorie, 1, 84
Blair, Richard Horatio, 65, 84, 87,
  89, 90
Blair, Richard Walmsley, 1, 146

Blunkett, David, 125
Böll, Heinrich, 131
Bonhoeffer, Dietrich, 108
Borkenau, Franz, 44, 74
  Spanish Cockpit, 42
Britten, Benjamin, 83
Buddicom, Jacintha, 3–4, 5, 89
Burmese Days, 8–11, 18, 23, 24
Burnham, James, 92
  Machiavellians, 97
  Managerial Revolution, 91
Burt, Sir Cyril, 124

Camus, Albert, 76
Cape, Jonathan, 64
Carlyle, Thomas, 94
Chamberlain, Neville, 67
Chase, James Hadley, 96
  No Orchids for Miss Blandish, 93–5
Chesterton, G. K., 26, 48, 71,
  110, 129–30
Christianity, 12, 21–3, 30–1, 39,
  54, 108, 110
Churchill, Sir Winston, 96
Clarion movement, 125–6
Clergyman's Daughter, 20, 23, 24,
  28–31, 34, 108
Coming Up for Air, 44, 45, 83
Common, Jack, 45
Connolly, Cyril, 43, 59, 67, 72
  St. Cyprian's School, 2, 24
Crick, Bernard, 11, 23, 37, 39, 43,
  58, 62, 63, 67, 85, 87
  developments in British

socialism, 127–8
Orwell's:
  Christiantiy, 21–3
  motivation as a writer, 16, 18
  school days, 4–5
Cripps, Sir Stafford, 74
'Critical Essays', 65
Crossland, Anthony, *Future of Socialism*, 129

Dakin, Humphrey, 3, 20, 87
Defoe, Daniel, *Robinson Crusoe*, 105
Deutscher, Isaac, 97
Dickens, Charles, 65, 110, 113, 131
  Orwell's essay, 72
Down and Out in Paris and London, 18–9, 21, 23, 25–8
Dunn, Bill, 86, 89, 91

Eliot, T. S., 64, 75
Empson, William, 61
Evening Standard (London), 60

Forster, E. M., 83
Freedom Defence Committee, 83
Freud, Lucien, 90
Fyvel, Tosco, 60, 63

Gissing, George
  Demos, Netherworld, 47
  New Grub Street, 32
Gollanz, Victor, 8, 21, 24, 36, 39, 40, 45, 64, 83
Gould, Bryan, 125
Green, Graham, *Brighton Rock*, 121
Greenwood, Walter, 40

'Hanging', 11–2
Havel, Vaclav, *Power of the Powerless*, 130–2
Hemingway, Ernest, 66

Hollis, Christopher, 6, 109
Homage to Catalonia, 42, 43, 54–6, 68–72, 107, 115
Home Guard, 59–60
Horizon, 59, 65, 67
'How the Poor Die', 18
Hunter, Lynette, *George Orwell: The Search for a Voice*, 27
Huxley, Aldous:
  Brave New World, 91, 98
  Point Counter Point, 120
Hyndman, H. M., 79
Hynes, Samuel, 111, 112

Independent Labour Party, 40, 42, 43, 46
'Inside the Whale', 46, 58, 72
intellectuals and totalitarianism, 92–5

Jacques, Eleanor, 21
John, Augustus, 83

Kafka, Franz, 103–4
Kateb, George, 97
Keep the Aspidistra Flying, 23, 24, 31–5, 39
Kirwan, Celia, 67
Koestler, Arthur, 43, 81, 83
  Darkness at Noon, 69, 82, 98, 130
  Gladiators, 59, 67, 82
Kopp, Georges, 42, 85
Kubal, David, 107
Kundera, Milan, *Book of Laughter and Forgetting*, 101, 103

Labour party and socialism, 123–9
Laski, Harold, 40
Lawrence, D. H., 38, 39, 119
League for the Dignity and Rights of Man, 83
Leavis, Q. D., 34

Lee, Robert, 10
Lewis, C. Day, 22
'Lion and Unicorn', 60, 73
Lloyd George, David, 54
London, Jack, 5, 16
    People of the Abyss, 17, 25, 38
Longhurst, Henry, 2
Luther, Martin, 99
Lyons, Euguene, Assignment in
    Utopia, 45, 91, 99

Mackenzie, Compton, 23, 35
McNeice, Louis, 61
Manchester Evening News, 67
Mann, Gollo, 94
Martin, Kingsley, 42
Marx, Karl, 24, 75
    Communist Manifesto, 76
Mayakovsky, V. V., 75, 76
Meacher, Michael, 125
Merleau-Ponty, Maurice, 90
Miller, Henry, 40, 45
Mitchell, Austin, 126
Morris, William, 52, 68, 124
    News from Nowhere, 71
Muggeridge, Malcolm, 84

National Council for Civil
    Liberties, 83
New Statesman (and Nation), 42, 44
Nineteen Eighty-Four, 21, 65, 67, 87,
    88–9, 91, 95–106, 107, 116–18

Obelisk Press, 45
O'Brien, Conor Cruise, 121
Observer, 62, 67
Ogilvie, David, 13
Orwell, Sonia, née Brownwell, 67,
    86
    death of, 91
    marriage to Orwell, 90

O'Shaughnessy, Laurence, 24, 43
    death of, 48

Partisan Review, 59, 74, 79
Peace Pledge Union, 44
Peters, Richard, 19
Plant, Raymond (Lord), 127–8
Plowman, Max, 22
Popper, Karl, 97
POUM, 40, 42, 71
Powell, Anthony, 84, 86
Priestley, J. B., 23

'Raffles and Miss Blandish', 93–4
Raleigh, Sir Walter, 100
Rees, (Sir) Richard, 19, 32, 37, 88,
    108, 121
Reilly, Patrick, 100, 106
Remarque, Eric Maria, All Quiet on
    the Western Front, 71
Road to Wigan Pier, 39, 46–54, 107,
    112–13, 118
Runciman, (Sir) Stephen, 5
Russell, Bertrand, 83
    Power: A New Social Analysis, 99
Russian revolution (1917), 77, 81

Salkeld, Brenda, 95
Sassoon, Siegfried, 38
Shaw, Bernard, 5, 81, 92, 94
    Major Barbara, 17, 52, 114, 126
Shelden, Michael, 1, 7, 13, 27, 42,
    58, 67
'Shooting an Elephant', 11
Sitwell, Osbert, 83
Small, Christopher, 106
Socialists, Orwell's critique, 50–4
Spanish civil war, 69–72
Spender, Stephen, 109
Stalin, Joseph, 75, 76, 77
Steiner, George, 128, 129
Straus, George, 62

'Such, such were the joys',
13–14, 15, 86–7
Swift, Jonathan, *Gulliver's Travels*,
64, 75
Symons, Julian, 84, 89

Tawney, R. H., 89
Time and Tide, Orwell as theatre
critic, 58, 59
Todd, Ron, 125
Toynbee, Arnold, 40
Tressell, Robert, *Ragged Trousered
Philanthropists*, 20, 48
Tribune
Orwell as:
editor, 62, 63, 67, 86
reviewer, 58, 60
Trollope, Anthony, 94
Trotsky, Leon, 75, 76, 77

Voltaire, 121

Warburg, Fredric, 61, 64, 65, 87,
88, 89
Watson, Susan, 84, 85
Webb, Sidney and Beatrice, 92
Weil, Simone, 121
Wells, H. G., 5, 53, 92, 97
West, Anthony, 86
Williams, Raymond, 14, 18, 28, 35
critique of Orwell's socialism,
40, 95, 107
Wodehouse, P. G., 66
Woodcock, George, 68, 91
Woolf, Leonard, 92
working class, 119–21
British, 46–54, 111–14
Spanish, 54–6, 69–70, 115

Zamyatin, Yevgeny, *We*, 63, 91